Che
Teashop

Jean Patefield

COUNTRYSIDE BOOKS
NEWBURY, BERKSHIRE

COUNTRYSIDE BOOKS
3 Catherine Road
Newbury, Berkshire

To view our complete range of books,
please visit us at
www.countrysidebooks.co.uk

ISBN 1 85306 840 3

Designed by Graham Whiteman
Cover illustration by Colin Doggett
Photographs and maps by the author

Produced through MRM Associates Ltd., Reading
Typeset by Mac Style Ltd, Scarborough, N. Yorkshire
Printed by J.W. Arrowsmith Ltd., Bristol

Contents

Introduction — 6

Walk

1 Thurstaston *(3 miles)* — 10
A short gem of a walk that cannot be too highly recommended
for its wildlife interest and outstanding views.

2 Delamere Forest *(5 miles)* — 16
An attractive walk exploring Delamere Forest and passing some
of the scientifically important sites of this special area.

3 Utkinton and the Sandstone Trail *(6 miles)* — 20
This walk explores the central part of the Way with excellent
views and a visit to a farm teashop.

4 Cotebrook *(3 miles)* — 25
This delightful short walk lies mainly within Little Budworth
Country Park but leaves to visit an excellent teashop

5 Shropshire Union Canal and Cheshire Farm *(5½ miles)* — 29
An easy level walk that includes an attractive stretch of the
Shropshire Union Canal, some good views of the Peckforton Hills
and a visit to Cheshire Farm, famous for its delicious ice cream.

6 Beeston Castle and Higher Burwardsley *(5 miles)* — 32
A charming walk dominated by two castles on the sandstone ridge
called the Peckforton Hills, with a visit to a busy craft centre for tea.

7 Acton and Nantwich *(5 miles)* — 36
An easy walk with considerable historic interest through some of
the richest farming land in the county and with varied waterside
walking, calling in at Nantwich and an interesting, modern teashop.

8 Hankelow and Audlem *(6 miles)* — 41
An easy, almost level walk, with a long stretch by the Shropshire
Union Canal, leading to the ancient town of Audlem and a
delightful traditional teashop.

9 Wybunbury *(5½ miles)* — 46
A varied and easy route through the classic English countryside
of South Cheshire, with gentle rolling meadowland, picturesque
meres and an abundance of trees, to an antiques centre for tea.

10 Hassall Green *(4 miles)* 51
A level walk, made possible by the transport systems of the past, to a teashop overlooking a canal.

11 Astbury *(4 miles)* 54
A short but immensely varied walk with something of everything that this part of Cheshire has to offer, calling in at a garden centre with an exceptionally good teashop.

12 Wildboarclough *(3½ miles)* 58
A short walk exploring one of the most attractive valleys in Cheshire's Peak District.

13 Rainow and Bollington *(5½ miles)* 62
Starting with an exhilarating ridge walk, this route to an excellent teashop in Bollington has considerable historic interest and excellent views.

14 Lyme Park *(5 miles)* 67
A varied and energetic walk in the Peak District, visiting one of Cheshire's great houses.

15 Macclesfield Canal and the Middlewood Way *(4½ miles)* 71
An easy, level walk, ideal for a lazy day and with a choice of two tea stops.

16 Hare Hill and Alderley Edge *(4 miles)* 75
A delightful walk exploring one of Cheshire's favourite beauty spots, with many wonderful views and a visit to a famous tearoom.

17 Knutsford and Tatton Park *(5½ miles)* 80
An exceptionally interesting walk with much to see along the way.

18 Dunham Massey *(4½ miles)* 85
A gentle, level amble that explores the Dunham Massey estate, two estate villages and the Bridgewater Canal.

19 Lymm *(3 miles)* 89
A charming short walk that explores the environs of the very attractive historic village of Lymm.

20 Budworth Mere and the Anderton Boat Lift *(4 miles)* 93
A short and easy walk crammed with interest, including a visit to a marvel of Victorian engineering, now restored to working order, and two possible tea stops.

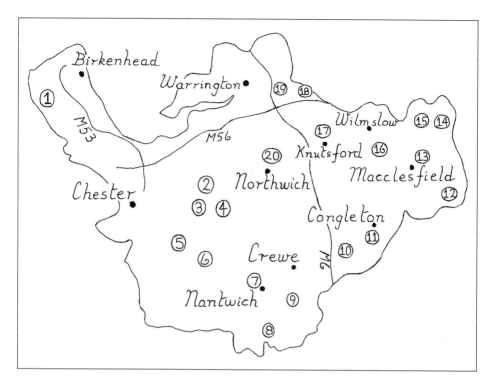

Area map showing the locations of the walks

Key to Sketch Maps

Path on route	— → — –	Teashop	
Path not on route	. . .	Pub referred to in text	PH
Road	═══	Point in text	⑤
Major river or canal	🌊	Car park	▢
Stream	∿∿∿	Building or feature referred to in text	▪
Lake or pond	☁		
Summit	▵	Railway	┼┼┼┼●┼┼┼
Church	†		

Introduction

No county can be more suited to a book of teashop walks than Cheshire. Local historians always pointed out that the shape of the county resembled a teapot with the Wirral as the spout and a panhandle of territory thrust to the east as a broken handle with the curve of the Mersey forming the lid. Since 1974 the teapot has become rather battered as bits have been removed and added by tinkering with local government boundaries. It was originally planned to dismember the county entirely but in the end the men in grey suits gave much of the Wirral to Merseyside and the broken handle to Greater Manchester. Wilmslow fought a determined and successful battle to remain part of Cheshire and the quintessentially industrial Lancashire towns of Warrington and Widnes were added. In the 17th century, before drinking tea became popular, Cheshire was said to resemble an outstretched eagle's wing. Now it is a rather amorphous squiggle on the map but retains its varied and interesting countryside with many attractive teashops.

There is an unusually wide range of landscapes to enjoy in Cheshire. The eastern extremity is part of the Peak District National Park with high moorland criss-crossed by drystone walls and dissected by steep cloughs or valleys with tumbling streams (walks 12 and 14). In the west the open expanses of the Dee estuary are host to vast over-wintering populations of wading birds that graze its rich mud flats (walk 1).

The central plain is rich farmland noted for its dairy herds that produce the milk from which the famous Cheshire cheese is made – and some delicious ice-cream (walk 5). Some say that the derivation of the name itself is Cheeseshire, though that is not true. Herds of placid dairy cows are a common sight and before the Second World War Cheshire was the most densely stocked dairy area in the world (see walk 7). The plain is broken by the sandstone of the Peckforton Hills (walks 3 and 6) and Alderley Edge (walk 16).

Cheshire lies between the great industrial areas of south Lancashire and the West Midlands and is crossed by the transport links between these two areas. The first were the canals. Commercial traffic has now ceased but they have gained a new lease of life from pleasure boats and, more importantly from the point of view of this book, they have bequeathed a legacy of towpaths. Many of the walks in this book (for example, walks 7, 15 and 19) include stretches of canalside walking on well-maintained level paths where watching the boats adds an extra dimension, especially where they pass through locks (walks 8 and 20).

The existence of great industrial and commercial conurbations so close has deeply influenced Cheshire. Any attractive area close to a source of wealth will tend to become a commuter area and so it has been with the northern parts of the county. This has led to snide references to the swell belt and to Cheshire being a little bit of Surrey that got lost up the M6. Nothing could be further from the truth. Cheshire has far richer farmland, a much longer history and a clearer sense of its identity with important cities, historic towns and villages and distinctive architecture.

Despite its proximity to great centres of population and rich farming, Cheshire has many areas of wildlife interest and ecological importance which are explored by the walks in this book. These include the Dee estuary and Thurstaston Common (walk 1), Delamere Forest (walk 2) and Little Budworth Common (walk 4).

Tea is often said to be the best meal to eat out in England and I believe it is a meal to be enjoyed on all possible occasions. The custom of afternoon tea is said to have been invented by Anna, Duchess of Bedford, in about 1840. She often became peckish in the late afternoon – don't we all? – and invited her friends to join her in a snack of sandwiches and cake. Scones with clotted cream and strawberry jam, delicious home-made cakes, toasted teacakes dripping with butter in winter, delicate cucumber sandwiches in summer all washed down with the cup that cheers are some of the best, typically English food available and often excellent value. Bad for the figure maybe, but the walking will see to that.

Tea is not only refreshing during a walk; it is good for you! In Scotland apothecaries sold it and it was available on prescription on form number 99. This is the origin of the name of one famous brand. Another, Typhoo, is the Chinese word for doctor.

The best teashops serve a range of cakes, all home-made and including fruit cake, as well as scones and other temptations. Teapots should be capacious and pour properly. Many of the teashops visited on these walks fulfil all these criteria admirably and they all offer a good cup of tea. They always have at least light lunches available as well so there is no need to think of these walks as just something for the afternoons.

There are many excellent establishments in Cheshire but even so, teashops are not scattered evenly throughout the county. In some places popular with tourists, the visitor is spoilt for choice. In such cases the most convenient teashop that, in the author's opinion, most closely fulfils the criteria set out above is recommended but should that not appeal, there are others from which to choose. In other places where there is a delightful walk to be enjoyed, the choice for tea is more limited. However, they all offer a good tea part way round an attractive walk. The opening times and telephone number of each teashop are given.

The pleasures of summer walking are obvious. Many of the teashops featured in this book have an attractive garden where tea can be taken outside when the weather is suitable. However, do not overlook the pleasures of a good walk in winter. The roads and paths are quieter and what could be better than sitting by an open fire in a cosy teashop scoffing crumpets that you can enjoy with a clear conscience due to the brisk walk to get them? Be aware that many teashops are rather vague about when they open out of season: it seems to depend on weather and mood. If you are planning a walk on a wet November Tuesday, for example, a call to check that tea will actually be available that day is a wise precaution. Some are definitely closed outside the summer season or during the week and for these walks, where possible, an alternative source of refreshment is given. In most cases, these are pubs serving food, which in some cases includes tea.

The twenty walks in this book explore the various landscapes of Cheshire. They are all between three and six miles long and should be well within the capacity of the average person, including those of mature years and families with children. They are intended to take the walker through this attractive corner of England at a gentle pace with plenty of time to stop and stare, to savour the beauty and interest all around. A dedicated yomper and stomper could probably knock off the whole book in a single weekend but to fully appreciate the countryside it is necessary to go slowly with your eyes and ears open. Some of the walks are short and level, ideal for a pipe opener on a winter's day, or giving plenty of time to dawdle away a summer's afternoon. Others are longer or more strenuous, some making an excellent all day expedition. Certain of the walks involve some climbing. However, this presents no problem to the sensible walker who has three uphill gears – slowly, very slowly and admiring the view. The hills add enormous interest but with no ascents, there are no views.

All the routes are circular and on public rights of way or permissive paths. They have been carefully checked but, of course, in the countryside things do change; a stile replaces a gate or a wood is extended. A sketch map illustrates each walk. An Ordnance Survey map is useful as well, especially for identifying the main features of views. The Explorer 1:25,000 (2$\frac{1}{2}$ inches to 1 mile) series is by far the best to use for walking. Sheets 257, 266, 267, 268 and 276 together with Outdoor Leisure 24 cover the walks in this book. The grid reference of the starting point and the appropriate maps are given for each walk.

Of course, it behoves us all to remember that the place where we take our recreation is other people's workplace and act with consideration to those who depend on the countryside for their livelihood and make their homes there.

Nevertheless, a right of way is exactly what it says – it gives a right of passage over what is otherwise private land. Landowners are not allowed to block a right of way but agricultural activities such as ploughing and harvesting sometimes of necessity obliterate footpaths and this is legal providing the path is restored within two weeks. Many farmers are conscientious about this and even where they are not, the walkers' feet will do the job on a well-used path. Problems can arise when a farmer does not restore a little-used path and crops grow up across the line. What is the walker to do? To walk round the edge of the field is technically a trespass and anyway is not always as easy as it sounds. The alternative is to keep to the line of the path and trample down the crops. This is what the law requires you to do, providing no more damage than absolutely necessary is caused, and yet this course of action often doesn't feel right. The solution in each case is a matter of common sense but it is always worth remembering when walking in the countryside that a right of way is not a concession but a prerogative and that footpaths and bridleways are part of this country's highway network.

The walks, all starting where a car can be parked, are designed so that the teashop is reached in the second half so a really good appetite for tea can be worked up and then its effects walked off. However, it sometimes fits in better with the plans for the day to start and finish at the teashop and so for each walk there are details of how to do this.

So put on your walking shoes and prepare to be delighted by the charms of Cheshire and refreshed by a traditional English tea!

Jean Patefield

Walk 1
THURSTASTON

This short gem of a walk cannot be too highly recommended. Almost all of it is across land owned by the National Trust or Wirral Council and encompasses both woodland and open heath, a blaze of purple blossom in late summer. It is not actually in Cheshire any more since much of the Wirral peninsula was lopped off the county by local government reorganisation. However, since it is within the historic boundaries of Cheshire, I decided to include it here. The route climbs easily to the sandstone ridge of Thurstaston Hill from where there are tremendous views stretching from the mountains of Wales to those of the Lake District, so be sure to choose a clear day.

Church Farm has an award-winning organic farm shop. One end has been made into a coffee shop, heated by a wood-burning stove in winter, and there are some tables outside for summer days. It serves a nice selection of sandwiches and delicious cakes – all organic, of course – as well as organic teas and coffees. The shop stocks a very wide selection of organic produce, including unusual cheeses such as Ribblesdale goats cheese so you might want to call again at the end of your walk to stock up. It is open throughout the year every day except Monday (open Bank Holiday Mondays) until 4.30 pm. Telephone: 0151 648 7838.

When the teashop is closed, the Cottage Loaf pub on the A540 serves food.

DISTANCE: 3 miles.

MAP: OS Explorer 266 Wirral and Chester.

STARTING POINT: Royden Park car park. GR 245858.

HOW TO GET THERE: From the A540, West Kirby-Heswall road, take the B5140, Montgomery Hill, towards Frankby and Greasby for ³/₄ mile. Turn right to Royden Park gates and follow the drive to the car park on the left. If that is full, there is further parking to the right of the drive.

ALTERNATIVE STARTING POINT: If you wish to visit the teashop at the beginning or end of your walk, there is a car park at Church Farm but permission should be sought before leaving a car for a long period. You will then start the walk at point 8.

THE WALK

1. Return to the entrance drive. Walk across it and ahead on a track past parking on the right. (If you use the parking to the right of the entrance drive, turn right along the track.)

2. At the end of the field on the right, turn left. Follow the main path round to the left as a path joins on the right. After a further 110 yards, again follow the main path round to the left and after a further 35 yards continue ahead on the left-hand branch, soon passing Hillbank House on the left, to a cross path and a metal seat on the right.

The lovely area this walk explores is almost all owned by the local authority or the National Trust. The original Hillbank House was a sandstone building constructed in 1865 and the surrounding grounds were laid out as gardens and park. Sir Ernest B. Royden erected the present house in 1931. This mock Tudor building was originally constructed at Bidston Hill in 1891 for a soap manufacturer and Sir Ernest had it moved to its present commanding location brick by brick. Following his death in 1961, Hoylake Urban District Council acquired the estate for use as a public open space known as Royden Park. Hillbank House is now a hotel and conference centre and not open to the public.

11

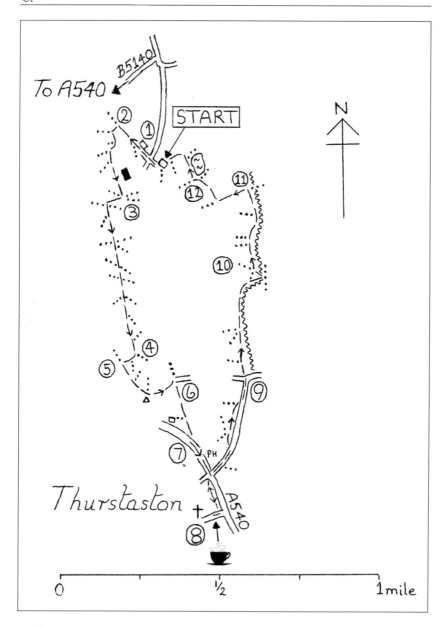

3. This is a complex junction of many paths. Standing by the seat and with your back to Hillbank House, take a path ahead, not that bearing right across an open area. After 75 yards this reaches a gate in a wall giving onto

Thurstaston Common, owned by the National Trust. Go ahead across the common, ignoring all paths to right and left and crossing at first one and then a second outcrop of bare sandstone.

In 1879 Birkenhead Glegg of Thurstaston Hall, together with two other prominent local landowners, petitioned to have Thurstaston Common enclosed. Birkenhead Council objected to this and requested that the highest and most attractive part of the common should remain unenclosed as a place of recreation. This proposal was finally agreed and 45 acres were ceded as public access land in 1883. The remainder of the common was divided between the landowners in return for loss of all commoners' rights. In 1916 27.5 acres of this land were given to the National Trust, with further donations since. The Common has been designated a Site of Special Scientific Interest as heath land is a rare and endangered habitat produced when early farmers cleared the original forest (see walk 4, page 27). The swathes of purple heather alive with the buzz and drone of many species of insects are a delight in late summer. If you examine the heather closely you will find that there are actually three different species present – true heather or ling, bell heather and cross-leaved heath. They are supposed to like slightly different conditions with cross-leaved heath preferring wetter conditions than true heather and bell heather being found in the driest circumstances but they often grow intermixed, as they do here. The ling has few leaves on the main shoots and the short side shoots bear four dense ranks of small leaves. The flowers are single and pale pinkish purple. The bell heather has leaves that can be tinged with bronze and curled over to protect the underside of the leaf. The leaves grow in a whorl or ring of three up the stem, each whorl giving rise to a leafy shoot. The flowers are a bit bigger than true heather, darker purple and are carried in a head or loose spike. The cross-leaved heath has its leaves in whorls of four and look quite grey because they are downy. The flowers are the largest of the three species, pink in colour and occur in a tight cluster at tips of the twigs. Gorse, which can have its bright yellow pea flowers at any time of year, grows among the heather. Remember the old saying 'kissing is in season when gorse is in bloom'.

4. At the end of the second outcrop, turn right on a cross path, slightly uphill, to another sandstone outcrop after 30 yards. Now bear right to reach the edge of a ridge in 50 yards.

During the Triassic Period, some 230 million years ago, the Wirral was situated approximately where the Sahara lies today some 15^0 north of

13

the equator and it was a desert with a windblown dune-like landscape. Over the eons of geological time the sand of the dunes was formed into stone and where it outcrops at the surface the dune formation is apparent.

5. Turn left along the ridge. Press on over the summit, passing a trig point, then shortly follow the main path round to the left and downhill to the end of a road.

On a clear day the views from Thurstaston Hill take in Black Combe in the Lake District 63 miles away, Carnedd Llewelyn in Snowdonia (40 miles) and Blackpool Tower (32 miles). The Dee estuary below is a crossroads of bird migration routes. These were established some 18,000 years ago as the glaciers retreated at the end of the last Ice Age. The mudflats may look like a barren wasteland but are actually an enormously rich habitat with as many as half a million worms and thousands of snails and cockles per square metre. Some species of migrating birds stop on the Dee on their way to and from their summer breeding grounds in the Arctic Circle while others remain all season and up to 120,000 birds can be seen on the estuary over winter. The Dee used to be an important shipping route when Chester was a port in Roman times but has been silting up for centuries and some day there will be just a river channel with dry land across to North Wales.

6. Turn sharp right along a sandy track to a gate onto a road.

The Romans first used this road, now the A540, to get from their garrison at Chester to an anchorage at Meols. Several Romano-British finds have been made in the fields adjacent to the road.

☕ **7.** Turn left. Go ahead over a crossroads and take the next road on the right, Church Lane, to the entrance to Church Farm and the teashop on the left.

Records of a church at Thurstaston go back to 1125 but the present building dates to 1885.

8. Turn right out of the farm to the main road and turn left to retrace your steps to the crossroads. Turn right along Thurstaston Road, signed 'Irby Pensby'. Shortly, opposite the entrance to Hill Farm, a path starts on the left that runs parallel with the road by the fence around Thurstaston Nature

Reserve. Several gates give access and it is worth going into the reserve in late summer when the display of heather blossom is breathtaking. However, the route lies parallel with the road outside the reserve and eventually rejoins and continues along the road.

9. When the main road bends right at the junction with School Lane, continue in the same direction on a path through a gate. When the path forks after 60 yards, take the right branch. Ignore all paths to the left. At a wooden footbridge on the right, follow the path round to the left to stay in the wood.

10. After some 60 yards, level with a bench on the left, turn right on an oblique cross path. Ignore all paths to the left to stay just inside the wood to a T-junction at the end of the wood.

As you walk through the wood, you will notice that though it is quite a small area, the mix of trees varies. In some places it is dominated by silver birch that have grown to replace the heath land as grazing has declined (see walk 4, page 27). Left alone this would spread all over the heath and would, in time, itself be replaced by oak woodland, so the heath has to be managed to stop this happening. In other areas the dominant trees are pines which developed from the plantations made when the estate was developed as a country residence.

11. Turn left. When the wall on the right ends, follow the path round to the right and then as it bears left past the track of a miniature railway.

12. Do not go ahead across the track and an open area but turn right to pass Roodee Mere on the right. This leads past the entrance to the Walled Garden on the left and then to the car park.

The Walled Garden is an attractive and peaceful place to rest before leaving. Information boards explain its history and the work that is being undertaken.

Walk 2
DELAMERE FOREST

This attractive walk explores Delamere Forest and passes some of the scientifically important sites of this special area. Much of the route is along tracks, which makes for easy walking, but it also uses smaller paths not so much on the beaten track, and passes two meres with contrasting histories.

Station House Café is housed in the former station buildings at Delamere and caters for any meal you might need during the day from the all-day breakfast through to lunch and tea. Lunch can be light or a full meal, including a choice of daily specials. For tea there is an excellent choice of cakes and pies served with lashings of cream if you wish. The interior is decorated with advertising memorabilia and there are some tables outside on an attractive, shady patio. It is open from 9.30 am to 5 pm every day throughout the year. Telephone: 01606 889825.

DISTANCE: 5 miles.

MAP: OS Explorer 267 Northwich and Delamere Forest.

STARTING POINT: Barnsbridge Gate picnic area car park. GR 542716.

HOW TO GET THERE: From the B5152, Frodsham to Tarporley road, at Hatchmere, take a minor road west, Ashton Road, from crossroads in the village, signed 'Manley Mouldsworth', for just under 1 mile to a car park on the left.

ALTERNATIVE STARTING POINT: If you wish to visit the teashop at the beginning or end of your walk, start in Linmere picnic area car park (charge). The teashop is through a gate at the end of the car park. Or use the train: Delamere station is on the Chester–Manchester line and adjacent to the teashop. You will then start the walk at point 10.

THE WALK

1. Walk to the far end of the car park and take the path ahead. Follow this round to the right to a T-junction with a major track. Turn left and walk for 120 yards.

Delamere Forest today is a tiny remnant of its former extent, when it stretched from Frodsham to Nantwich and from the Weaver to the Gowy. It was not all wooded; there were areas of open heath, as well as meres and mosses. After the Norman Conquest the term 'forest' did not mean the dense woodland the word conjures up today. When an area was declared a forest it meant that it was set aside as a hunting preserve and draconian regulations were imposed on ordinary people to preserve the beasts of the chase - deer and boar.

2. Turn right, slightly downhill, and follow the path to a T-junction with a track.

3. Turn left for 150 yards to a track junction then turn right. This shortly runs parallel with a railway.

4. At a cross path turn left across a bridge over the rail track. Over the bridge, follow the main path bearing left.

5. At a T-junction turn left.

6. Some 25 yards before a bridge back across the railway there are two small paths on the right. Take the first, which shortly leads to Black Lake. Turn left beside the lake. At the end of the lake bear left. The path may be overgrown but press on to shortly reach a T-junction with a cross path. Turn right and follow this path to another T-junction.

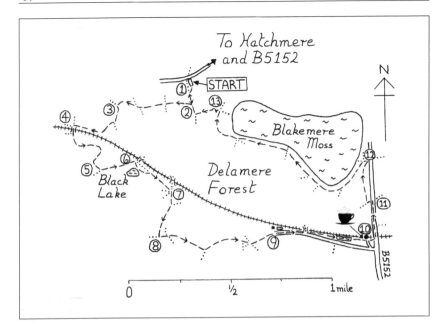

Cheshire has many of these shallow lakes and ponds, often called meres. They have developed in natural depressions in the glacial drift left by the ice sheets that covered the Cheshire plain some 15,000 years ago. On a geological time-scale, they are temporary features in the landscape as over time they become filled with peat and form a moss. Sometimes the lake becomes covered by a raft of floating vegetation, producing a quaking bog known as 'schwingmoor'. Black Lake has been selected as a Site of Special Scientific Interest because it is a very early stage of schwingmoor development. All stages from open water to more or less consolidated schwingmoor, with trees living on it, can be seen. A notice board nearby explains the history of Black Lake, together with a chart to identify the fourteen species of dragonflies and damselflies that have been recorded.

7. Turn right, then immediately take the left-hand one of three paths. At the top of a rise bear right, through a wooden barrier. Follow this path down into a dip and up the other side to a T-junction, with a track at the edge of the forest.

8. Turn left. At a cross track reached shortly, continue ahead, signed 'Linmere Delamere Station'. Walk along the track to Linmere Lodge Visitor Centre.

Gradually hunting became less fashionable. After Edward I, James I is the only monarch to have hunted in Delamere, and then for just one day. The growing pressure for agricultural land led to widespread assarting, the ploughing of forest land. The Crown did not really try to stop this, instead aiming to make a profit by imposing heavy fines, which they did not always find easy to collect. The end came in 1812 when what was left was officially disafforested. The Crown retained some land and this is still farmed as crown property and some was reserved for the Surveyor of Woods and Forests and planted with conifers.

9. Take the drive from the Visitor Centre. At a bridge over the railway, bear left off the drive on a path between the railway and the drive. Press on through a car park to a gate into the teashop garden at the far end.

10. From the teashop go across the access road to the station and up some steps to a road. Turn left.

11. Opposite the entrance to Whitefield car park on the right, turn left on an unsigned path that meets a broader cross path after 25 yards. Turn right to continue parallel with the road to a cross track opposite the exit from the car park on the other side of the road.

12. Turn left down to the mere and follow the main track as it bears left to walk by the mere. When it forks, bear right and ignore all paths to left and right to carry on round the mere. Eventually the track is somewhat further away from the mere but press on ahead to reach an attractive small picnic site.

The mere is Blakemere Moss. It started life as a shallow lake that became filled with peat over the centuries forming a wet, boggy area called a moss. It was eventually covered with trees. Wetlands are an important and threatened habitat for many species so in 1996 the decision was made to restore it. The trees were cleared and it was flooded in 1998. The water level is controlled by a sluice gate near Station Road.

13. Turn left, signed 'Blakemere Trail Delamere Way'. Take either fork as they shortly rejoin and follow the path up to a T-junction with a track. Turn right to rejoin the outward route and retrace your steps to the start, turning right to the car park after 220 yards. (If you started at Delamere Station, turn left after 100 yards.)

Walk 3
UTKINTON AND THE SANDSTONE TRAIL

The Sandstone Trail is a 34-mile long path traversing the sandstone ridge that thrusts out of the Cheshire Plain. This walk explores the central part of the Way and has extensive views of the Welsh mountains to the west and the Peak District to the east. The welcome teashop sits beside the Sandstone Trail and the return after refreshment is a most attractive path just inside part of Delamere Forest.

 Summer Trees is an excellent farm teashop next to the Sandstone Trail. It fully caters to the needs of walkers. There are substantial sandwiches, toasted if you wish, and baguettes, all with a salad that is rather more than a garnish. Alternatives for lunch include omelettes, quiche and things on toast. There is a tempting choice of cakes or scones served with jam and cream. A selection of walking and other magazines is provided for you to read whilst taking your refreshment. For warmer days there are some tables outside overlooking the attractive garden. Summer Trees is open

every day except Monday (open Bank Holiday Mondays) and Friday all year between 11 am and 5 pm. Telephone: 01829 751145.
There is no other source of refreshment on this walk.

DISTANCE: 6 miles.
MAP: OS Explorer 267 Northwich and Delamere Forest.
STARTING POINT: Tirley Lane parking area for Primrosehill Wood, Delamere Forest. GR 549666.
HOW TO GET THERE: From the B5152, Cotebrook-Frodsham road, about a mile north of the A49 at Cotebrook, take Heaths Lane, signed 'Utkinton 1¼, Kelsall 4'. Continue ahead at a junction, signed 'Kelsall 2½' for about ¼ mile to an informal lay-by on the right at the junction with Tirley Lane, signed 'Utkinton ¾'.
ALTERNATIVE STARTING POINT: If you wish to visit the teashop at the beginning or end of your walk, there is a car park at Summer Trees but permission should be sought before leaving a car. There is very limited roadside parking near the teashop. You will then start the walk at point 10.

THE WALK
1. Walk along Tirley Lane, signed 'Utkinton ¾' for about half a mile to a school on the left. Cross a road and continue ahead along Northgate. When the lane ends, carry on in the same direction down some steps and follow the path round to the right for 35 yards to a small wooden kissing gate on the left.

Utkinton is a small village with some modern houses for commuters. Yet nearly 400 years ago, for a short time, Utkinton was as busy a place as any in England, attracting as many as 2,000 people daily. What brought them here? To find the answer to that question you will have to complete the walk!

2. Turn left through the gate. Walk uphill to shortly reach a small gate and then bear half left to a stile. Press on diagonally across the next field to a stile in the far left corner. Walk along the left-hand side of the next field and ahead to find a stile by a gate onto a lane.

3. Turn left for 100 yards then turn right at a T-junction. Cross Utkinton Road and keep on along Fishers Green, ignoring a lane on the left. At the end of the lane carry on along a track, slightly left for 75 yards to a signpost for the Sandstone Trail, where the track bends left.

The farm at the T-junction is Utkinton Hall. It was the home of the Done family, High Foresters of Delamere Forest. It was their duty to accompany

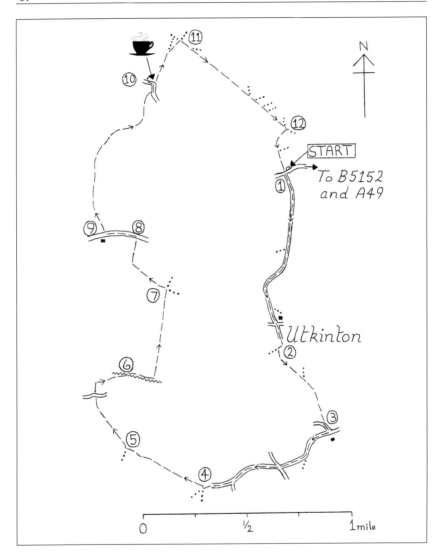

the monarch when he came to hunt in the Forest and the ancient horn
that was their badge of office is now in Chester Museum. The last
monarch to exert his hunting rights was James I (see walk 2, page 19)
who knighted John Done after killing a stag.

4. The route now joins the Sandstone Trail, which leads to the teashop and
is well waymarked with yellow circles containing a black arrow and

footprint enclosing a black 'S'. Go over a stile to the right then head diagonally across a field to a stile in the far right corner. Over the stile follow the path along the right-hand side of a field to a stile on the right. Over this stile continue in the same direction, now on the left-hand side of a field, to a stile onto a track.

The Sandstone Trail is 34 miles long and runs from Frodsham to Whitchurch, winding between the sandstone ridges, forests and rolling countryside of Cheshire's western side. Another beautiful stretch is explored on walk 6, page 32.

5. Turn right and follow the track to a lane. Cross the lane and continue in the same direction over a stile and then along the left-hand side of a field to a pair of stiles and a footbridge.

6. Over the second stile turn right. At the end of the field follow the boundary round to the left. At the end of this large field keep ahead on a track to stiles on either side of a gate.

7. Go over the stile on the left then walk with a hedge on the right. At the end of the field, cross a stile on the right and walk along the left-hand side of a field to a road.

8. Turn left.

9. Some 30 yards after the entrance to Rock Farm, turn right along a track and follow this up to a lane. Turn left to the teashop on the right after 50 yards.

10. Return to the lane and turn left back along the lane to find a path on the left next to the teashop building. Follow this to a gate on the left. Go through the gate and continue in the same direction for a few yards then bear half right to a stile by a small wooden gate giving on to a cross path inside woodland.

11. Turn right. When the path forks take the right branch to stay at the edge of the wood. Stay on the sometimes narrow path just inside the wood, ignoring all paths to the left, to a track.

This wood is a fragment of Delamere Forest – see walk 2, page 16 for more information. It is now managed for commercial forestry, nature conservation and public enjoyment.

12. Turn right for 10 yards, then turn right again on a path, still just inside the wood. At a track continue in the same direction back to the lane where this walk started.

Just near here is a spring known as Whistlebitch Well because the water 'whistled' as it came out of the ground. Some 400 years ago, one John Greenway of Utkinton was afflicted with fits and was apparently cured by the water from the well. As news of this spread, people came from all over the north of England to seek cures for their ills and soon as many as 2,000 people a day were flocking to the village. We are told about this in a pamphlet published in London in 1600 that includes details of forty reputed cures. These included, 'One Robert Bradley, who came out of Darbishire [sic] the 24. of July, being borne at Chappell in the Frith, was led hither blind, hath here recovered sight, and the fourth of August is gone home without leading.' *The numerous visitors to the well must have brought prosperity to the village, with so many people needing board and lodging and proper provision was made to receive such an influx of the sick and the curious. Initially this had official support but after three years Master Done closed the forest to all outsiders and Utkinton's chance to become a famous spa was gone forever. The official reason given was that the invasion was causing disturbance to the queen's deer but there is some suggestion that the use of the well had religious overtones and that was unacceptable in times of such delicate religious sensitivities. Today the spring rises into a small locked brick-built structure, and is piped a few yards into a holding tank, from whence it is pumped to provide the water supply of Primrose Hill, a house in the wood, which was formerly a hunting lodge.*

Walk 4
COTEBROOK

This is a delightful short walk that is a joy at any time of year. Much of the route lies within Little Budworth Country Park encompassing woodland and the most important area of lowland heath in Cheshire so there is considerable ecological interest. We leave the country park to visit Cotebrook, home to a charming teashop, for refreshment before the shorter return leg, also through woods and across heath. There are some interesting seats carved from fallen logs at the start and near the end of this highly recommended route. The proximity of this walk to Oulton Park motor racing circuit means that it is a more peaceful experience in winter.

Cotebrook Coffee Shop offers a selection of superb cakes made by a local lady keen on baking and her enthusiasm shows. There are also scones and toasted teacakes. For lunch there is a choice of sandwiches, toasted if you wish, with tempting and tasty fillings – all very simple, but delicious. There are tables inside, in an airy conservatory, and outside, so there is somewhere comfortable for all weather. The Coffee Shop is open throughout the year every day except Monday between 10 am and 4 pm. Telephone: 01829 760144.

There is no alternative source of refreshment on the route but there are pubs in Cotebrook and Little Budworth.

DISTANCE: 3 miles.

MAP: OS Explorer 267 Northwich and Delamere Forest.

STARTING POINT: Little Budworth Country Park car park. At the time of writing this is locked at 7 pm. GR 590654.

HOW TO GET THERE: From the A49, Warrington-Tarporley road, a quarter of a mile south of its junction with the A54, take a minor road, Coach Road, south-east, signed 'Oulton Park 1½ Little Budworth 1¾' for just over a mile to a car park on the left.

ALTERNATIVE STARTING POINT: If you wish to visit the teashop at the beginning or end of your walk, start in Cotebrook on the A49, where there is a car park by the teashop. You will then start the walk at point 6.

THE WALK

As you approach the car park along Coach Road you will notice the impressive gatehouse of Oulton Park ahead. Oulton Park was one of the great stately homes of Cheshire. The Egerton family rebuilt their ancient hall in the 18th century and surrounded it with a magnificent park. The hall burned down in a disastrous fire in 1926, probably started by an electrical fault. Seven people, who were among those trying to rescue some of its treasures, were killed when the burning roof collapsed. It was not rebuilt and the park was used as a military camp during the Second World War. After the war the roads became the basis for the famous motor racing circuit that can attract large crowds in the summer.

1. Take a footpath from the rear of the car park by a notice-board and innovative carved map and follow the path ahead, pausing to admire a superb carved seat on the right after 20 yards. Carry on through a gate and over a drive and a track, following maroon waymarks.

2. Some 150 yards after crossing the track turn right, still following the maroon waymarks. Go ahead on the main path at a complex junction, soon going gently downhill, to a small pond on the left.

This is an important area of lowland heath, a rare and declining habitat. Prehistoric farmers cleared the primeval forest from areas such

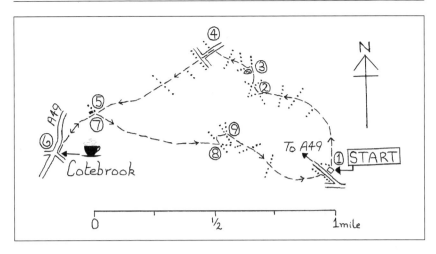

as this, where the light sandy soils could easily be cultivated by primitive wooden ploughs. Robbed of the protective forest canopy the fragile soils deteriorated rapidly into impoverished acid soil, incapable of supporting agriculture. Grazing and the depredations of rabbits all helped to maintain the habitat by nibbling any saplings that managed to grow. This grazing pressure has declined with changes in agriculture and the effects of myxomatosis so the tree cover has greatly increased. If you study the trees, you will see there are few large and therefore old specimens and there are many silver birches. Birch is a pioneer species. The trees don't live all that long - perhaps 100 years - but they alter the environment by allowing nutrients to accumulate in the soil, paving the way for other species, such as oak, to colonize. Without management, the heath would eventually revert to the oak woodland from which it was formed with the loss of the unique wildlife that depends on it.

3. Immediately after the pond, turn left for 30 yards, then bear right uphill away from the pond. Some 20 yards after the top of the slope, follow the path round to the left, then on through an old car park to a lane.

4. Turn left. Cross a road and continue ahead on a signed path along a track. Ignore a path with maroon waymarks on the left after 150 yards as we now leave the nature trail that has guided us to this point.* Press on ahead at a cross track.

* There are some magnificent beeches on the right of the track. Beech is a lovely tree with smooth, grey bark and glossy green leaves. It is

27

especially beautiful in the spring, when the newly emerged leaves are so fresh, and in autumn when they change from gold to orange to brown. Southern England is the northernmost extent of the beech's range: individual trees such as these are found further north, often planted for their ornamental value, but there are no extensive beech woods.

☕ **5.** When the track bends sharp right in front of a house, continue ahead on a hedged path. ** Note this point. At a main road turn left to the teashop on the left a few yards along Oulton Mill Lane.

Cotebrook is a hamlet strung out along the A49. The name derives from the Anglo-Saxon for an animal enclosure beside a brook.

6. Turn right out of the teashop and right along the main road then turn right along the footpath to retrace your steps to the point ** noted above.

7. Cross a stile on the right and head across the corner of a field to another stile. Over this bear slightly right to a stile by a gate then press on in the same direction along the right-hand side of two fields. Now bear slightly left across the next field to find a stile by a gate onto a track.

8. Turn left along the track for 30 yards. Fork right towards a field entrance and after a further 20 yards turn right through a gap in a fence into woodland. Follow this path for 75 yards to a five-way junction.

9. Take the second path on the right, waymarked by the familiar maroon arrows. Follow this to a T-junction. Turn right and almost immediately left to a road and the car park directly opposite.

Little Budworth Common is a good place for a fungus hunt in the autumn. One species you might see is Slippery Jack. It has a distinctive bright brown cap covered with a layer of slime when it is fresh. This dries out as the fruiting body matures. It is supposed to be edible, but I wouldn't try it. The taste is said to be nothing much and some people have been known to have violent allergic reactions after eating it.

Walk 5
SHROPSHIRE UNION CANAL AND CHESHIRE FARM

This walk is centred on one of the richest farming areas in Cheshire and some of the milk and cream is used to make truly scrumptious ice cream at Cheshire Farm. This easy level walk includes a visit and makes its way there along an attractive stretch of the Shropshire Union Canal and quiet lanes and tracks. There are some surprisingly good views of the Peckforton Hills crowned with the dramatic silhouettes of Beeston and Peckforton castles. The return is similar and there is the option of a useful short cut if all the ice cream you have sampled proves too much!

Cheshire Farm is a rural ice cream factory making its delicious ambrosia from the produce of the surrounding lush countryside. It includes the Country Kitchen tea rooms, which offer an excellent choice of cakes and cream teas. Light lunches are also available such as sandwiches and filled jacket potatoes, with a choice of daily specials such as quiche and salad. Next door to the tea room is the real highlight of a visit – the ice cream parlour where you can sample one or more of over thirty varieties of delicious ice cream. I particularly liked the gooseberry fool, which was wonderfully creamy and rich, yet with a refreshing fruity tartness. And I did enjoy the mocha as well and... They are open between 10 am and 5.30 pm in summer and 10.30 am and 5 pm from October to April. Telephone: 01829 770446.

DISTANCE: 5¹/₂ miles.

MAP: OS Explorer 267 Northwich & Delamere Forest and 257 Crewe and Nantwich.

STARTING POINT: Crows Nest Bridge on Shropshire Union Canal. GR 495605.

HOW TO GET THERE: From Tiverton on the A49, Tarporley–Whitchurch road about two miles south of Tarporley, take a minor road west signed 'Tiverton ¹/₄ Huxley 3 Tattenhall 6'. At Huxley turn left along Huxley Lane, signed 'Hargrave 1³/₄ Tattenhall 3 Chester 7'. At a T-junction turn left, signed 'Tattenhall 2¹/₄' for half a mile to informal parking areas either side of a bridge over a canal.

ALTERNATIVE STARTING POINT: If you wish to visit the teashop at the beginning or end of your walk, there is a large lay-by on the lane opposite Cheshire Farm. You will then start the walk at point 5.

THE WALK

This is the Shropshire Union Canal (see walk 8, page 43). This part, originally known as the Chester Canal, is the oldest and was completed in 1779.

1. From the bridge go down to the towpath and turn right. Walk beside the canal to the third bridge, number 110.

2. Go over a stile just before the bridge and go ahead across a field to a footbridge over a stream. Carry on across a second field to find a stile allowing you to cross a railway. Over the railway track go ahead to a stile in the far right corner of a third field.

3. Turn right along a tiny lane and continue ahead when it shortly becomes a track after passing a farmhouse. Ignore a track on the right and continue over the railway. At one point the track is permanently flooded and the right of way is diverted into a field on the left for a short distance. Carry on under the railway, after which it becomes a lane once more.

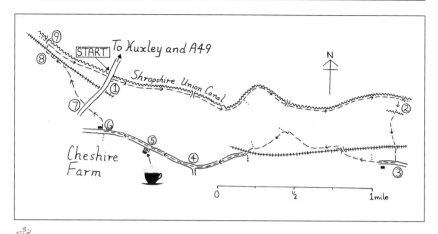

4. At a T-junction turn right to the teashop on the left after about a third of a mile.

In 1986 Tom and Margaret Fell decided to use the milk produced by their 300 cows to make a delicious ice cream using whole milk and 48 per cent double cream. In July that year the ice cream parlour opened to the public and was an instant success. It now has over 250,000 visitors a year.

5. Turn left out of Cheshire Farm and continue along the lane.

6. Immediately before some cottages turn right on a signed path. The path is not visible on the ground: the right of way goes across a field then turns left to walk with a hedge on the right to a stile in the corner of the field onto a road.

Note: the next part of the route involves navigating slightly awkward stiles and parts of it can be overgrown and nettle-infested in summer. If you wish, you can cut the route short at this point by turning right along the road and this leads back to the start.

7. Cross the road and take a path more or less opposite, signed 'Hargrave'. Follow the path along the right-hand side of three fields.

8. Just after the end of the third field go over a stile and across the railway track. Over the track, press on through a patch of scrub and down a very short but steep slope to reach the canal again at bridge 114.

9. Turn right by the canal to the next bridge and the start of the walk.

Walk 6
BEESTON CASTLE AND HIGHER BURWARDSLEY

This charming walk is dominated by two castles on the sandstone ridge called the Peckforton Hills. Their histories are very different: one is the genuine article while the other is a 19th-century facsimile. A visit to the former, Beeston Castle, where this route starts, is highly recommended before or after your walk. The views are unparalleled and it is of considerable historic interest. It is not surprising that it is one of Cheshire's most visited sites. Field paths, tracks and lanes lead to Higher Burwardsley and tea. The return uses the Sandstone Trail, along a delightful track, with extensive views across the Cheshire Plain.

 Higher Burwardsley, nestling in the flanks of the Peckforton Hills, is home to Cheshire Workshops. They sell all kinds of candles and you can watch them being made. Other crafts are on display as well, with a wide range of goods for sale in the gift shop. They also run popular workshops for children. Chandler's Restaurant serves breakfasts between 10 am and noon followed by lunches until 2 pm, then teas until 4.30 pm so you can be sure of nourishment whatever time of day you choose to do this walk. Choices for lunch range from tasty sandwiches, such as salmon, roast pepper and rocket, through salads and filled jacket potatoes to hearty full meals. For tea you can choose from traditional goodies such as flapjack, Eccles cake or shortbread as well as cakes. Or you might be tempted by a Warming Dream – hot chocolate topped with marshmallows, cream and chocolate flake. Chandler's Restaurant is open throughout the year. Telephone: 01829 770401.

DISTANCE: 5 miles.

MAP: OS Explorer 257 Crewe and Nantwich.

STARTING POINT: Sandstone Trail car park at Beeston Castle. GR 539589.

HOW TO GET THERE: Follow the signs for Beeston Castle from the A49, Tarporley–Whitchurch road, The car park is on the left, just before the castle. The car park on the right, a couple of hundred yards further on, is for visitors to the castle only.

ALTERNATIVE STARTING POINT: If you wish to visit the teashop at the beginning or end of your walk, start in Higher Burwardsley, where there is ample parking at the Cheshire Workshop. The teashop is at the rear of the car park. You will then start the walk at point 5.

THE WALK

Beeston Castle is perched on a rocky summit 500 ft above the Cheshire plain and it is well worth the climb to the ruin for the fabulous views of the Pennines to the east and the Welsh mountains to the west, and for its historic interest, enhanced by the small museum at the entrance which explains the site's history. The castle is now in the care of English Heritage and is open throughout the year from 10 am until 6 pm or dusk. Telephone: 01829 260464.

1. Turn right out of the car park to return along the lane. At a T-junction turn left, then left again at the next T-junction. After 130 yards turn right, signed 'Bunbury' for 230 yards.

2. At a left-hand bend turn right along a track signed 'Peckforton'. This shortly leads to a cross track. Go over this and the stile next to a field gate and bear right across a field in the direction shown by the arrow on the waymark, passing to the left of a tree-fringed pond to find a stile into a wood. Continue in the same direction through the trees then on across

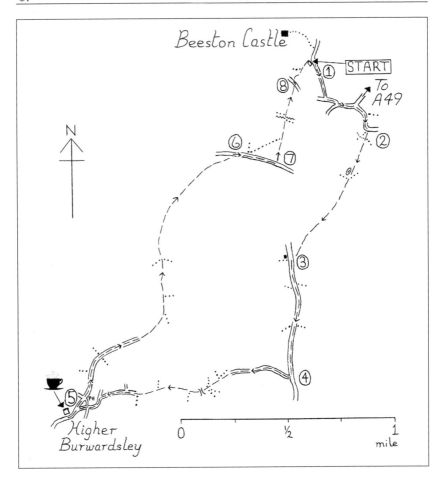

another field, now heading towards a turreted lodge seen ahead, to a stile in the far right corner onto a lane.

The imposing castle dominating the hill ahead is Peckforton Castle, a complete fake. It was built between 1844 and 1851 as a home for John Tollemach, member of Parliament for Cheshire 1841-1872 in the style of a 12th-century castle. Too big to live in or even keep warm, it has had a chequered history in recent years. It makes a more realistic medieval backdrop than many genuine castles and has been used many times as a film set, including episodes of 'Dr. Who'.

3. Turn left for about half a mile.

☕ **4.** Turn right on a tiny lane. Press on when this becomes a cobbled track and then when it becomes a lane again, ignoring all side turns, until it eventually leads downhill to Cheshire Workshops and the teashop at the rear of the large car park.

The way is called the Elephant Track, a reference to a life-size stone elephant that used to stand in the garden of one of the cottages. The bridge across the track once carried the main carriage entrance to Peckforton Castle. This area is supposed to be haunted by a servant woman from the castle who is said to carry a severed head beneath her arm.

5. Turn left out of the teashop car park. Bear left at the first junction and continue ahead at cross roads, passing the Pheasant public house. When the lane ends, press on through a gate on a track that shortly becomes part of the Sandstone Trail (see walk 4, page 20), waymarked by a black footprint in a yellow circle. Follow this delightful track for about a mile to a lane.

6. Turn right. Ignore the first signed path on the left and continue to a second.

7. Turn left. Follow the path down the left-hand side of a field to a footbridge then on across a second field to a lane.

There are excellent views of Beeston castle from here. The castle did not see action until the Civil War when the Parliamentarians garrisoned it mainly as a store for arms and provisions. A devout Puritan and cheese factor called Steele who had no military experience was put in charge. The Royalists were busy at Nantwich (see walk 7, page 39) and could not spare the men to mount a siege. One daring officer and eight soldiers were sent to attempt a surprise raid. They scaled the crag and were probably admitted by a traitor. Despite the fact that he had 60 soldiers at his disposal, Steele surrendered the fortress. He was allowed to march his garrison to Nantwich with the honours of war. The senior military were not impressed. They threw him in prison and later had him shot. At his final confession he denied treachery and was most worried about an illicit affair he had carried on with a maid at one of the local inns. After the surrender of Chester in February 1646, orders were given for Beeston's defences to be destroyed. This 'slighting' of Beeston was made all the more thorough by the victorious Parliamentarians due to their earlier humiliating defeat at the castle.

8. Turn left for 40 yards then right to continue on the Sandstone Trail. This leads back to the car park where this walk started.

Walk 7
ACTON AND NANTWICH

This part of Cheshire is some of the richest dairy farming land in Cheshire. In the 1960s it was said there were more cows in a 10-mile radius of Nantwich than anywhere else in the world! Things have changed a bit in the last quarter of a century but there is still the lush, green landscape, with many fine trees giving a parkland feel. This easy, more or less level walk starts in an ancient village that was the site of a significant battle in the Civil War. It then explores this richness on the way to Nantwich and an intriguing tea stop. As with so many Cheshire walks there is plenty of waterside walking with stretches by the river Weaver, a spring-fed lake once reputed to have medicinal properties and, to round it off, the Shropshire Union Canal.

Curshaws occupies an ancient building that originated as cottages in the early 17th century. Soon afterwards, in 1676, it was converted into almshouses for widows of the town. It now represents an intriguing combination of ancient and modern with a fresh, contemporary interior including a conservatory leading out onto an attractive patio. It perhaps gives us an idea of what teashops will be like in the 21st century as it reinterprets the concept in a very modern way. The traditions are not ignored with a cream tea, toasted teacakes or a delicious selection of cakes available. For a light lunch there is an enterprising range of tapas, wraps or hot sandwiches served with salad and chips. For the really hungry full meals are served between noon and 2.30 pm. These are complemented by very tempting puddings such as cappuccino flavoured crème brûlée served with hazelnut ice cream. They are open from 9.30 am until late during the week and from 11 am on Sunday throughout the year. Telephone: 01270 623020.

DISTANCE: 5 miles.
MAP: OS Explorer 257 Crewe and Nantwich.
STARTING POINT: Acton village car park. GR 632530.
HOW TO GET THERE: Acton is on the A534, Nantwich-Wrexham road, and the car park is about 60 yards south of the church on the opposite side of the road.
ALTERNATIVE STARTING POINT: If you wish to visit the teashop at the beginning or end of your walk, start in a car park on First Wood Street in Nantwich signed from Welsh Row and close to the bridge on the Acton side of the town. The teashop is on Welsh Row, to the right. You will then start the walk at point 9.

THE WALK
1. Return to the road and turn left.

Acton is a small village with a big church, well worth a visit. The present building is on the site of an earlier Saxon church and dates from about 1180 with many later additions and changes. The black basalt font is Norman and has had a chequered history. It was thrown out during Puritan times when such things were out of fashion and was used on a local farm as a pig trough. Next it became a garden ornament at nearby Dorfold Hall before being recognised and restored to the church in 1897. There are fine monuments to the Wilbraham family and interesting carved stones surviving from the earlier Saxon building. An unusual feature is the ledge round the walls. This was a bench provided for those too infirm to stand in the days before churches had pews. Hence the saying, 'the weakest go to the wall'. In the churchyard is the grave of Albert Hornby, who died in 1925. He was captain of the England cricket team of 1882 who played so badly against the Australians that the bails were ceremoniously burned and preserved in a little urn, played for since as the Ashes.

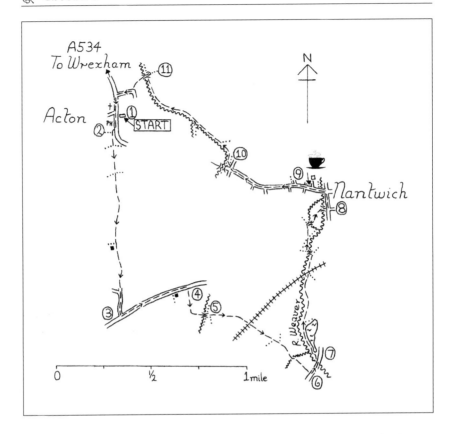

2. Some 50 yards past the Star pub, turn right on a signed path along a track and almost immediately fork left. Walk along the track and continue ahead when it eventually becomes a surfaced lane to reach a T-junction with a road.

3. Turn left. Ignore a signed path on the right at farm buildings and continue ahead for a further 165 yards.

4. Turn right along a surfaced track.

5. Immediately after crossing a bridge over a canal, as the track turns right, go ahead through a small gate next to a field gate. Walk along the right-hand side of a field. At the end of the field, go along a short stretch of path and across the railway track. Carry on along the right-hand side of a second field then the left-hand side of a third field to find a footbridge over a stream

about 100 yards to the right of the left-hand corner of the field. Walk across the next field to a pedestrian gate onto a road.

6. Turn left, using the footway on the opposite side of the road.

7. Immediately after crossing the river Weaver bear left off the road to find a footbridge over a branch of the river on the left after about 40 yards. Cross this then turn right on a riverside path.* Follow the path under a railway bridge then cross the river at a footbridge. Over the bridge turn right to continue in the same direction on a surfaced path. When the path forks turn right to cross a branch of the river and follow this to a road.

* Shrewbridge Lake on the right is fed by the river Weaver and a brine spring. In the fields on the left was Shrewbridge Meadow salt works built in 1693 before Nantwich's salt industry started to decline. The lake used to be overlooked by the Brine Baths Hotel, which attracted visitors from far and wide to the healing power of the brine spring.

8. If you wish to explore Nantwich go ahead up Mill Street. Otherwise, turn left to traffic lights. Turn left along Welsh Row to the teashop on the right.

Nantwich is one of the most picturesque and historic towns in Cheshire and well worth taking the time to explore. It was the principal salt town from Roman times until the 17th century but after that the decline was rapid and production had ceased by the middle of the 19th century. The town has certainly seen action. It was devastated by the Normans because of its resistance to the Conquest, repeatedly attacked by marauding Welsh, suffered destruction by fire in 1438 and again in 1583 and was subject to bombardment in the Civil War. It narrowly escaped catastrophe in 1944 due to the heroism of 23-year-old American pilot Arthur Brown. He stayed at the controls of his blazing Thunderbolt fighter and steered it away from the town, crashing near Shrewbridge Lake. The town maintains a memorial to this brave airman. The Elizabethan look is largely due to the rebuilding that took place after the fire in 1583. It burned for 15 hours and the fire fighting efforts of the townspeople were not helped by frightened bears, released by the landlord of the Bear Inn as the flames approached his property. Only three major buildings survived the conflagration, one being the huge church with its many interesting and amusing medieval carvings.

9. Turn right out of the teashop and walk along the road to a bridge over the road.

This is Welsh Row along which Welsh farmers used to drive their cattle to Nantwich market. There are many fine timber-framed and Georgian buildings on either side of the road.

10. Go up steps next to the bridge to a canalside path. Turn right beside the canal to the second bridge, number 93.

This is the Shropshire Union canal (see walk 8, page 41). During the Civil War Nantwich was garrisoned by the Parliamentarians and defended by fortified trenches. The Royalists brought in their toughest troops, under the command of Lord John Byron, to take the town. First he tried to break the morale of the defenders by bombarding the town with red-hot shot. When this failed he attempted a dawn assault that was bloodily repulsed. Finally he tried to starve them out and this was on the point of success when a relieving force arrived. The battle was mainly fought in the fields to the right. The Royalists were based at Dorfold Hall at Acton and at Beambeath. Unfortunately for them, the river Weaver burst its banks and destroyed their bridge. This forced the troops at Beambeath to make a six-mile round trip via the bridge at Shrewsbridge to reinforce their colleagues at Acton. The Parliamentarians broke out of Nantwich and attacked the Royalists from the rear. With fewer troops than expected and attacked on both sides, the Royalists were defeated leaving Cheshire, apart from Chester, in the hands of Parliament. Nantwich still celebrates this famous victory by re-enacting the battle and wearing a sprig of holly on Holy Holly Day, which takes place on the Saturday nearest to 25th January, the date of the battle in 1644.

11. Leave the canal path and cross the canal. Follow the path ahead into Acton and continue along the road to a T-junction. Turn left back to the start.

There was fighting round Acton during the battle, including in the church itself. Some of the 1,800 prisoners, of whom 120 were women, were kept in the church overnight and the dead were buried in Dead Man's Field in the village. The vicar was so concerned he reputedly buried the altar vessels for safety. He took the secret of their hiding place to his grave and they haven't been seen since.

Walk 8
HANKELOW AND AUDLEM

This easy, almost level walk explores the rich countryside at the extreme south of the county, where the Cheshire Plain meets the hillier terrain of Shropshire. The centrepiece is a long stretch by the Shropshire Union Canal, passing the first three in a series of 15 locks that carry boats up to the higher ground. Much entertainment may be had watching them, with seats conveniently placed to enjoy the spectacle. The canal is often on an embankment and the towpath has remarkably good views for little effort. It leads to the ancient town of Audlem and a delightful traditional teashop, much patronised by cyclists. The return is a pleasant stroll by lanes, tracks and field paths to Hankelow.

The Old Priest's House is situated in a quaint old building opposite the church in Audlem. It has a charming, old-fashioned atmosphere and serves generous slices of delicious cake as well as other teatime favourites such as scones and toasted teacakes. For a light lunch there are sandwiches and filled jacket potatoes, with home-made soup if you wish, and these are intended to satisfy the hungry cyclist and walker. There are also daily specials such as, on my visit, poached salmon steaks or paella. And don't forget the home-made ice cream! They are open every day between 10 am and 5 pm except Tuesday throughout the year. Telephone: 01270 811749.

When the teashop is closed there are pubs in Audlem that serve food, notably the Shroppie Fly overlooking the canal.

DISTANCE: 6 miles.

MAP: OS Explorer 257 Crewe and Nantwich.

STARTING POINT: Hankelow village green. GR 671454. There are several spots round the village where a car can be left without causing inconvenience, notably down Hall Lane.

HOW TO GET THERE: Hankelow is on the A529, Nantwich-Audlem road, about 1½ miles north of Audlem.

ALTERNATIVE STARTING POINT: If you wish to visit the teashop at the beginning or end of your walk, start in Audlem, where there is ample parking in a public car park in Cheshire Street. Turn right out of the car park to find the teashop opposite the church. You will then start the walk at point 7.

THE WALK

1. With your back to the main road and the White Lion, and facing the pond, take a lane to the right, Hall Lane. Follow this as it goes round to the right.

2. At the end of the surfaced road, turn left over a stile on a signed footpath – the South Cheshire Way. At the time of writing this is not visible on the ground but lies along the left-hand side of the field. At the end of the field, cross a stile and carry on ahead for a short section within the hedge and then along a track on the right-hand side of a field. Follow this to a bridge over the river Weaver.

3. Over the bridge turn left, following the South Cheshire Way waymark. With the river on the left, walk to a stile. Over the stile head up the left-hand side of two fields, again following the SCW waymarks. Now head half right across the next field to a metal gate about two thirds of the way along the right-hand side of the field. Go through the gate and turn left to a stile. Over the stile, go ahead across two fields to a lane.

4. Turn left for about 200 yards then turn right on a signed path along a track to a bridge over a canal.

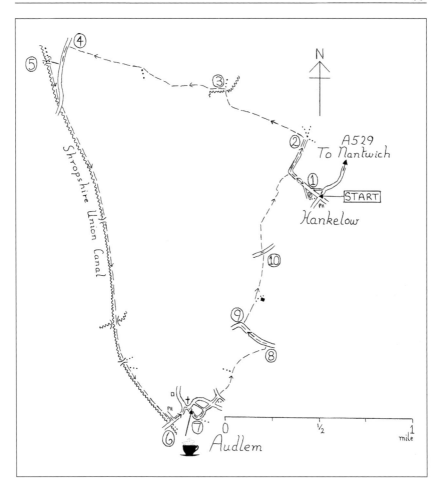

5. Immediately before the bridge go through a gate on the right and down to the canal. Turn left along the towpath and follow this for about 2 miles to a road just past the Shroppie Fly.

The full name of this canal is the Shropshire Union Canal Main Line. It is part of the Shropshire Union Canal System, formed in 1846 when the constituent canals were amalgamated and run by the Shropshire Union Canal & Railway Company. This branch, linking Wolverhampton with the river Mersey, has been described as the last trunk canal route to be built in England. It was completed in 1835 and was the last major civil engineering accomplishment of Thomas Telford. The Shroppie fly-boats

43

were famous. These craft, which operated on other canals too, ran non-stop, day and night delivering important and perishable goods. Worked by four-man crews, the elite of boatmen, they changed horses on the move and ran to a strict timetable. They had priority over all other traffic, except passenger packets, which took absolute precedence. The Shroppie Fly used to be a warehouse and was converted to a pub in the 1970s. The bar is half an old narrow boat.

6. Turn left into Audlem to the teashop on the right opposite the church.

Audlem is a most attractive small town with a 13th-century parish church perched on a mound and towering over the centre. This has a couple of interesting features. Resting on a plinth in the Lady Chapel is a Roman funerary urn made for the ashes of Titia Charis and her husband Titus Marius Alexander. It is decorated with their portraits and her hairstyle suggests it was made in about AD 100. It was brought from Rome to Audlem by a former vicar. On the south wall is a mass dial. This is a stone with a hole to take a stick. There are scratches to act as a sundial and it was a primitive timepiece to enable the priest to know when to say mass in the days before clocks. The stone seems to have been turned upside down during a restoration. There is more information about the church available inside. The structure below the church that looks rather like a bus shelter is the old butter market, in use into the 20th century. Next to it is a glacial boulder called the bear stone. This has a ring set into the top and the unfortunate animals were apparently tied to it during bear baiting, part of the market entertainment in more brutal times past.

7. Walk down Vicarage Lane next to the teashop and follow it round to the left*, joining another lane, to a main road. Cross the road and continue ahead along Salford. Ignore a track forking right. As the road bends left, turn right along a track, Mill Lane, to effectively carry on in the same direction. When the main track bends left, carry on in the same direction along a hedged path to a lane.

*On the left is the 17th-century grammar school, now enjoying a new lease of life as accommodation for the elderly. It is unusual because it was built during the troubled times of the Civil War and subsequent Commonwealth. Thomas Gamull, a local man who became a wealthy grocer in London, left £500 to build the school. The principal executor

was his cousin, who was an ardent Royalist so had his estate confiscated by Parliament. He used the bequest to augment his war chest. After the war, two of the local trustees who had been on the Parliamentary side managed to get the money released and so it was built as intended. Its most distinguished pupil was Sir Stapleton Cotton, who received his elementary education here. He went on to have a brilliant and unusually long military career including fighting under Wellington at the Battle of Salamanca. He was created a peer for his services, becoming Viscount Combermere, and was also Governor General of Barbados and Commander-in-Chief of both Ireland and India. He took great pride in his achievements and Thackeray caricatured him in his work The Book of Snobs *as Sir George Tufto, whose 'breast sparkled with innumerable decorations'. His widow and biographer did not think the 'inefficient tuition' he received at Audlem School had much to do with his later glittering success.*

8. Turn left.

9. As the lane bends left, turn right along the drive to The Parkes. When the drive approaches the house, bear left off the drive to a stile into a field and walk along the left-hand side of the field to a main road.

10. Turn left for 20 yards, then turn right up some steps to a stile into a field. Follow the path along the right-hand side of three fields to a gate some 30 yards to the left of the far right corner of the third field. Go through the gate and to a track. Follow this to a lane and turn right back into Hankelow.

Walk 9
WYBUNBURY

*Y*ou *do not need to travel to Pisa to see a leaning tower. Cheshire has one of its own at Wybunbury and this walk starts there. It is a varied and easy route through the classic English countryside of south Cheshire, with gentle rolling meadowland, picturesque meres and an abundance of trees. While not completely flat, there are no serious climbs. Nonetheless, this is best thought of as a walk likely to take most of a day as the tea stop is bound to delay you for an hour or two at least because it is situated within the largest antique and craft centre in the area with several barns full of antiques and collectables of all kinds as well as craftsmen at work so you may find yourself spending some time looking round.*

The Dagfield Centre has two places to eat. The tearoom serves cakes and other teatime favourites as well as light lunches of sandwiches and filled jacket potatoes. There is a traditional interior and some tables outside

46

in a pleasant courtyard that was once the stable yard of the farmhouse. The superb Cheshire Farm ice cream (see walk 5, page 29) is also sold from one of the stables so be sure to leave a corner for some. In one of the barns is the restaurant, the Collectors' Kitchen, which also serves fuller meals, including a daily roast. Both are open throughout the year from 10 am until 5 pm. Telephone: 01270 841336.

DISTANCE: 5¹/₂ miles.

MAP: OS Explorer 257 Crewe and Nantwich.

STARTING POINT: Wybunbury tower. There is some parking by the tower or around the village, notably a small, informal layby just south of the tower at the junction with Wrinehill Road. GR 700498.

HOW TO GET THERE: Wybunbury is on the B5071 south from Crewe about half a mile north of its junction with the A51.

ALTERNATIVE STARTING POINT: If you wish to visit the teashop at the beginning or end of your walk, start at the Dagfield Centre where there is a large car park, though permission should be sought before leaving a car. You will then start the walk at point 8.

THE WALK

The tower is all that still stands on the original site of St Chad's church. St Chad was the first Bishop of Mercia and he was canonised after his death in AD 672. The first church is supposed to have been built on the place where he preached. Sadly, this was an unfortunate choice as the geology is very unstable and quite unsuitable for a large, heavy building. There have been five churches on this site since the 7th century. The tower was built in 1470 and has been straightened several times. The last church on this spot was constructed in 1893. At the consecration it was said, 'Nothing but an earthquake will ever move Wybunbury church again.' This confidence was misplaced and by the middle of the 20th century it was again unsafe. This time the village gave in and a replacement was built on a different site in the village. Most of the building was demolished in 1976 but the villagers formed a trust to preserve the landmark tower, which was last underpinned in 1989. Note the bishops on either side of the main door. Perhaps it is not surprising they look so depressed when you think of all this church has endured!

1. Facing the front of the tower, turn left along a footpath made of gravestones, the first being that of Martha, wife of Samuel Sutton, who died in 1763. Leave the churchyard through a kissing gate and follow the path

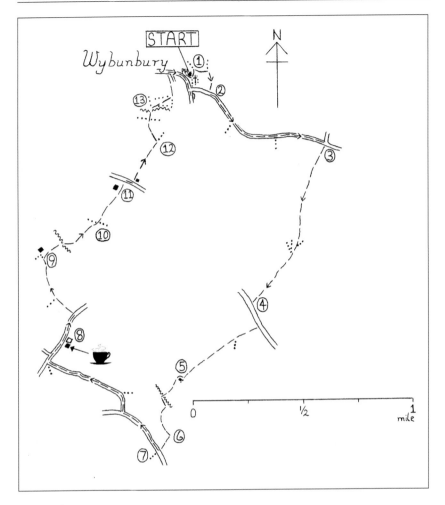

down a short slope. At the bottom turn right to a track. Turn right along the track to a lane.

2. Turn left along the lane for about ½ mile, ignoring two paths on the right.

3. Opposite Cobbs Lane turn right on a signed bridleway. Follow this to a track and continue ahead to a road.

The track leads through, at the time of writing, semi-derelict farmland and shows what can happen to the countryside if it is not farmed.

Fortunately, this is only a small area but illustrates why farming has an importance beyond food production and why we all depend on farmers to preserve the landscapes we love.

4. Turn left for 200 yards then turn right along a track opposite an informal layby. When the main track bears left, continue ahead.

5. Just before a modern house cross a stile on the right and bear left across a field to another stile. Over this stile turn left. The path soon leads down into a small valley and across a footbridge. Over the bridge turn left and walk round the left-hand perimeter of the field.

As you walk along this path it is interesting to compare the ecology of the two sides. On the left is a small wood that resembles what would be growing all around here on this light, sandy soil without human influence while on the right is a field that illustrates what human activity has made of it.

6. By an isolated oak tree turn right to walk with a fence on the left to a lane.

7. Turn right. Take the first lane on the right to a T-junction. Turn right to the Dagfield Centre and teashop on the right.

8. Return to the road and turn right for 180 yards. Turn left along the drive to Oat Eddish Farm.

9. Some 50 yards before the farm buildings turn right over a stile and head across a field to a footbridge over a stream. Now follow the path, crossing a stile, to arrive at a stile on the left.

10. Over this stile go ahead to find a double stile and footbridge. Now continue in much the same direction passing to the right of buildings to a stile onto the A51.

11. Turn right for 75 yards then turn left on a path along a track immediately before Thatcher's Cottage, an attractive black and white building with a roof to match its name. When the track ends continue in the same direction to the left of a hedge.

12. About 100 yards before the end of the field bear left across the corner of the field to a stile. Over this stile walk down the left-hand side of a field to a track. Cross the track and yet another stile and carry on down to a footbridge over Wybunbury Brook.

Wybunbury Brook was once used as a source of power for corn milling and iron production. Tie beams to hold Audlem church (walk 8, page 44) together after earthquake damage in 1777 were made here. Today it is a pretty spot with swathes of pink and white Indian balsam blooming by the stream in late summer. This species, although rather pretty, has escaped from gardens, has naturalised along rivers and canals and become a pest. Its other name is Jumping Jack. The seed pods dry out unevenly and burst open explosively when they are ripe to scatter the seeds as widely as possible. The slightest touch on a ripe capsule will fire it off most entertainingly.

13. Over the bridge turn right, first by the stream and then bearing away from it towards Wybunbury Tower to find a metal kissing gate in the top right-hand corner of the field. This gives on to a fenced path that leads into the village. Turn right back to Wybunbury Tower.

The unusual name of this village, pronounced 'Winbury', is probably a corruption of 'Wigbeorn's stronghold' and it was an important centre in Saxon times. On early maps it is shown as one of the most important settlements in the county.

Walk 10
HASSALL GREEN

The story of this walk is the changes in transport and the way redundant infrastructure has found a new lease of life as a place for recreation. The outward leg makes use of a most pleasant path along the route of a disused railway. A few steps bring you to a canal, with a teashop overlooking a lock, and the canal path is used for much of the return. The demands of train and canal means that the way is level and the going easy. Unusually for the walks in this book, the outward leg is slightly shorter than the return. This is because the views are better this way round.

Brindley's Lockside Restaurant takes its name from the engineering genius who pioneered England's canal network. It is above the Canal Centre shop and also has many tables outside so you can watch the boats rise and fall beside you. The shop and house were built at the same time as the canal in 1777, and the navigators who constructed the canal were paid in tokens that could only be exchanged in the Canal Company shop here. The shop has catered for working boatmen, and now holiday boats, continuously for more than 220 years and these premises also once housed the local bakery and the stables for the horses that pulled the laden barges.

Brindley's offers a full restaurant menu that stretches from breakfast to dinner with all the stops in between. For tea this includes teacakes and cream teas. Or you could indulge in what they admit are disgustingly fattening home-made puddings in mega-calorie portions with lashings of cream. Light lunches include filled baguettes and jacket potatoes or you could try something from the starter menu such as Camembert baked with wine. They are open seven days a week from 10 am to 4 pm, Telephone: 01270 762266.

DISTANCE: 4 miles.

MAP: OS Explorer 268 Wilmslow, Macclesfield and Congleton.

STARTING POINT: Lawton Heath End, where there is a lay-by on the B5078 next to the equestrian centre. GR 795570.

HOW TO GET THERE: The B5078 leads north from Alsager and south from the A533 Sandbach-Kidsgrove road.

ALTERNATIVE STARTING POINT: If you wish to visit the teashop at the beginning or end of your walk, start in Hassall Green where there is some street parking. The teashop is by the canal. You will then start the walk at point 5.

THE WALK

1. Facing the road, turn right along it. When the main road bends left, continue in the same direction, signed 'Hassall Green 2'.

2. Opposite Cherry Lane turn right on a path signed 'Salt Line'. Follow this delightful level path, for $1^1/_3$ miles, crossing a lane after just over a mile.

3. Some 30 yards after a signed path on the left, turn right on a signed path that shortly leads up to a stile. Continue along the left-hand side of a field to a track.

4. Turn left to reach a road then right along the road, over the canal to the teashop.

The startling pink church, St Philip's, started life as St Mary's, Alsager. In 1883 it was moved by horse and cart to its present location in Hassall Green. It is also referred to affectionately as the Tin Tabernacle.

5. Cross back over the canal at the lock and turn left to walk with the canal on your left for about $1^1/_3$ miles to bridge 141.

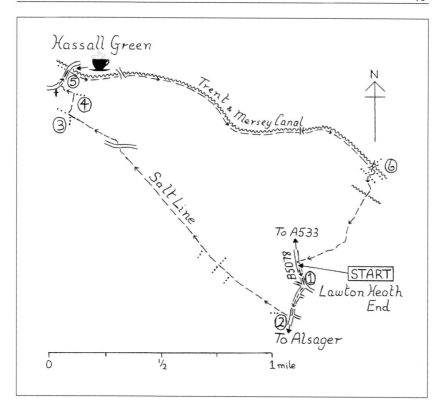

Completed in 1777, the Trent and Mersey Canal links the Bridgewater Canal near Runcorn with the river Trent, 93 miles away. Designed by the great canal engineer James Brindley, it was one of the earliest major canals in the country. Hassall Green lies halfway up 'Heartbreak Hill', where thirty locks lift the canal from the Cheshire plain to Harecastle Hill near Stoke-on-Trent.

6. Turn right. Immediately go over a cross track and ahead across a field to find a stile by a metal field gate. Now follow a narrow and possibly somewhat overgrown path as it bears slightly left and down to a remarkably substantial footbridge. Continue up the other side of the small valley to a gap. Press on along the right-hand side of two fields, cutting across the corner of the second field to a stile. Carry on across two small fields to a drive and gateway onto the road almost opposite where this walk started.

Walk 11
ASTBURY

This walk may be short but it is immensely varied, with something of everything this part of Cheshire has to offer - an exceptionally pretty village, ancient tracks, quiet field paths, woodland, a lane shaded by English oaks, a canal path and even a short stretch across the manicured greens of a golf course. Add to that a garden centre with an exceptionally good teashop and what more could you want for an attractive half-day excursion?

 If you get off to a really early start on this walk you might be in time to enjoy breakfast, served until 11.30 am, at the Garden Room Coffee Shop at Astbury Meadow Garden Centre. The excellent choice for lunch includes Staffordshire oatcakes (we are not that far from the border here), sandwiches or filled jacket potatoes, a selection of salads and daily specials. To complete lunch or for tea there are some excellent cakes and tempting dessert specials. They are open every day between 10 am and 5 pm in the summer, closing at 4 pm once the clocks have gone back. Telephone: 01260 276466.

DISTANCE: 4 miles.

MAP: OS Explorer 268 Wilmslow, Macclesfield and Congleton.

STARTING POINT: Astbury church. There is some parking by the church or, if that is full, there are other spots by the village green or village hall where it is possible to park without causing inconvenience. GR 846615.

HOW TO GET THERE: Astbury is just off the A34, Congleton to Kidsgrove road, about a mile south of Congleton.

ALTERNATIVE STARTING POINT: If you wish to visit the teashop at the beginning or end of your walk, start at the garden centre where there is ample parking in the car park. Permission should be sought before leaving a car for an extended period. You will then start the walk at point 8.

The Walk

The view of Astbury village green, covered with daffodils in spring, backed by the unusual church and surrounded by picturesque cottages, is deservedly one of the best known and most photographed images of Cheshire. Steps lead up to the massive 17th-century gateway and into the churchyard, which has a yew thought to be one of the oldest in England and some ancient stone monuments. One is a priest on a coffin lid, another a knight and a second knight lies with his lady under a battered canopy. The present structure is mainly 14th and 15th-century and is unusual because it kept its old north tower when a new west tower was added in the 15th century. The imposing spire was added some 300 years later. There has been a church here since before the Norman Conquest. The builders re-used materials from the previous structure and fragments of older carved stones can be spotted in the walls. They used the glass from the old church to make a damp-proof course and bits are exposed in the south wall where it has weathered.

1. Take the road between the church and the Egerton Arms. Turn left along School Lane and walk to the end.

2. Bear left on a drive and after a few yards, at the entrance to a house, bear right on a path that shortly leads into a field. Continue ahead across the field to a gap in the hedge and a stile. Over the stile bear slightly right to walk with a hedge on the left to a metal kissing gate on the left. Through the gate follow a short stretch of fenced path to a surfaced track.

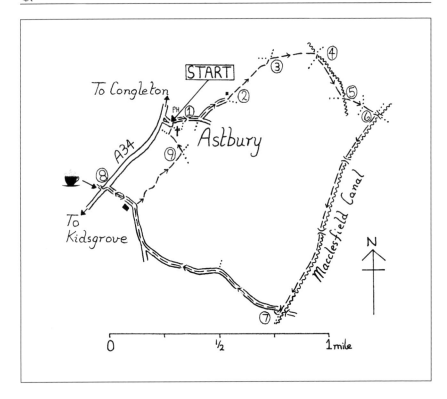

3. Almost immediately bear right through a gate onto a signed, fenced path and follow this to a footbridge over a stream.

4. Cross the stream, the Howty, then immediately cross back over an adjacent footbridge to a stile. Over the stile bear left to walk up the left-hand side of two fields above the steep-sided valley of the Howty, then continue down to another footbridge. Now follow the path up some steps to emerge on a golf course.

Ahead you can see what appears to be a ruined castle perched high on a hill. This is Mow Cop, another of Cheshire's famous landmarks. In fact, the 'castle' is a folly built in 1754 as a summer picnic shelter for Rode Hall and to improve the view. None of the walks in this book pass it but it is well worth visiting for the tremendous views across several counties.

5. Go more or less straight ahead across the course to a track and a path that continues in the same direction into woodland and marked by a yellow arrow on a post. This leads to the Macclesfield Canal (see walk 15, page 72).

6. Turn right along the canal path and follow it under two bridges.

7. Some half a mile after the second bridge the canal intersects a lane at an aqueduct, where the canal passes over the roadway. This is not at all obvious but, immediately after passing over the lane, turn right over a stile giving onto a steep path down to the lane. Turn left and walk along the lane to a main road, the A34, and the garden centre and teashop across the road.

8. Retrace your steps across the A34 and back along the lane to just past a farm on the right. Turn left along a path marked at the time of writing by a broken sign. Walk along the right-hand side of the first field to an obscure and rather overgrown stile in the far right corner. Continue in the same direction, closing with a hedge on the left, to pick up a track on the left-hand side of the field.

9. Near the end of the field, turn left over a stile then head over to the right-hand side of the field to find a stile into a field beside Astbury church. Walk the length of this field, then turn right on a hedged path that leads back to the front of the church.

People have lived here since time immemorial. Bronze Age remains have been found as well as evidence of a much later Roman camp and settlement. Interestingly, we know that the manor was held by one Wulfgeat before the Norman Conquest and yet Astbury is not mentioned by name in the Domesday Book. This is probably because it appears as Newbold, the name of the site of the manor. Down the centuries the parish has had its share of characters. One of them apparently had a beard over eleven feet long that he used to hang over an apple tree to dry after washing.

Walk 12
WILDBOARCLOUGH

Carved by a fast-flowing river, the Clough Brook, and with an abundance of mainly young trees, Wildboarclough is one of the most attractive valleys in the Peak District National Park. It is overlooked by one of the few true peaks in the Peak District, Shutlingsloe, the 'Matterhorn of Cheshire' – a shapely conical peak which rises steeply to the west of the village. Though Shutlingsloe looks impressive from the valley of Clough Brook, at 506 metres it's really little more than a pimple. This route climbs up the valley side for some excellent views before contouring round and down again to return by the river, passing the teashop.

The aptly named Brookside is housed in a whitewashed grit-stone cottage with tables outside and a traditional interior. The afternoon teas are substantial and include sandwiches, scones and cakes. Possibilities for lunch go all the way from well-stuffed sandwiches to full meals such as steak and kidney pie or mixed grills. They are open between noon and 4.30 pm on Saturday and Sunday all year. Telephone 01260 227632. When the tea shop is closed the Crag Inn, passed at point 5, serves food.

DISTANCE: 3¹/₂ miles.

MAP: OS Outdoor Leisure 24 The Peak District.

STARTING POINT: Nab Quarry car park near Wildboarclough. GR 973680.

HOW TO GET THERE: From the A54, Congleton–Buxton road, 4¹/₂ miles east of its junction with the A523, take a minor road north signed 'Wildboarclough 1¹/₂' to Nab Quarry car park on the left after ³/₄ mile.

ALTERNATIVE STARTING POINT: If you wish to visit the teashop at the beginning or end of your walk, there is a large lay-by outside the teashop. This is on the right further along the road past Nab Quarry car park. You will then start the walk at point 6.

THE WALK

1. Turn right out of the car park along the lane.

2. When the lane turns left at a junction, continue in the same direction on a smaller lane, past Lower Nabs Farm, for about half a mile.

3. Turn right on an unsigned surfaced drive that leads sharp right, almost back on yourself. Follow this as it slopes up the hillside for about half a mile.

4. When the drive bends sharp left take a signed path on the right and follow this sometimes indistinct path from gate to gate as it first goes slightly down and then contours round the hill before descending again to a lane at the Crag Inn.

As you descend the path Shutlingsloe is visible to the left. Also, look ahead and slightly right to see Crag Hall. In the 19th century this belonged to Lord Derby, who came here when he wanted to retreat from the troubles of the world. He once retreated so far that he missed an important meeting with Queen Victoria. To prevent such a faux pas happening again he had the offices of one of the mills turned into the biggest sub post office in England so telegraph messages could be sent to him. Winston Churchill also used Crag Hall as a country escape during the Second World War because of this facility.

 5. Turn right along the lane to the teashop on the left.

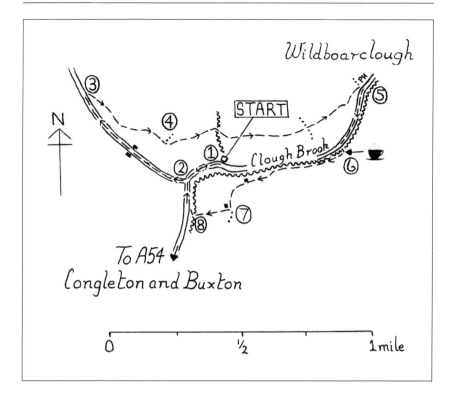

Wildboarclough

START

Clough Brook

N

To A54
Congleton and Buxton

0   ½   1 mile

Although it is difficult to imagine today, this quiet valley was once home to three mills using the power of the river. This was where James Brindley (see walk 19, page 92) first showed his engineering genius. His boss was employed to build machinery for a new mill but really was not up to the task and the assembled machinery would neither fit nor work. As the incompetent work proceeded it became known locally that the project was a farce and a waste of money. Brindley decided to rescue the project. One Saturday he walked the 25 miles to Manchester, persuaded a mill owner to let him spend Sunday inspecting similar machinery so he could devise a solution to the problems and then walked back. The whole design was revised according to Brindley's instruction, parts being rejected and rebuilt, others being redesigned and completely new improvements introduced. The work was brought to a successful conclusion, within the contractual time allowed, to the entire satisfaction of the proprietors of the mill. His technology was in use until 1952 after which it was, unfortunately, not preserved.

6. Return towards the lane but before crossing the river turn left on a signed path beside the river. Continue on the path as it veers away from the river after about a quarter of a mile to follow a wall on the right. Pass to the left of a cottage, after which the path becomes a track.

We are told that this valley takes its name from the fact that it was one of the last strongholds of wild boar in England. It is also one of several places where the last wolf is said to have been killed. It is certainly remote enough but I wonder if that is the true explanation. On 24 May 1989 there was a tremendous thunderstorm over the moors that caused a flash flood to rip through the valley, uprooting trees and sweeping away bridges, stone walls and the letterbox, which was never found. Bore is an old word for a racing river and there are earlier records of similar floods so perhaps the name really means 'wild racing river in the valley'.

7. Some 35 yards after the second building on the right, turn right on a path signed 'Owlers Bridge'. Walk down a field to a stile and footbridge over the river.

8. Over the bridge turn right to a lane and continue in the same direction. At a junction follow the lane round to the right to rejoin the outward route back to the car park. (If you started at the teashop, turn left at the junction to continue the route from point 2.)

Walk 13
RAINOW AND BOLLINGTON

The imposingly named Saddle of Kerridge is a finger of grit stone pointing to Bollington where the hills of the Peak District meet the rest of Cheshire. The views are outstanding and the walk along the ridge from Rainow to Bollington is particularly satisfying. The recommended route takes the climb up to the ridge in two stages separated by a delightful path that contours the hill. After the exhilaration of the ridge walk, the way drops down to Bollington for tea. The return leg is a pleasant stroll on an easy field path along the side of a hidden valley.

The Bollington Tea Rooms combine the best of a traditional teashop with a modern twist. I do suggest you try to time your walk to have lunch as they offer a delicious and innovative choice of substantial open sandwiches such as local ham with sweet mustard ketchup. For the smaller appetite there are tasty tapas, such as peppers stuffed with feta cheese served with bread, or olive oil and balsamic vinegar with garlic and onion bread. The tempting cakes are made locally and a popular choice is apple pie with cream and raspberry coulis. Other teatime goodies include crumpets, toasted teacakes and cinnamon toast. They are open every day, except Monday, from 9.30 am Tuesday to Saturday and from 11 am on Sunday. Telephone: 01625 578140.

When the teashop is closed there are several pubs in Bollington that serve food.

DISTANCE: 5¹/₂ miles.

MAP: OS Explorer 268 Wilmslow, Macclesfield and Congleton.

STARTING POINT: Sugar Lane, Rainow. GR 947762.

HOW TO GET THERE: From the B5470, Macclesfield–Whaley Bridge road, at Rainow, turn into the village along Round Meadow opposite the church. Bear left along Sugar Lane to find some roadside parking on the left where cars can be parked without causing inconvenience. Should this be full, there are other suitable parking spots around the village.

ALTERNATIVE STARTING POINT: If you wish to visit the teashop at the beginning or end of your walk, there is ample parking in Pool Bank car park opposite the teashop. You will then start the walk at point 11.

THE WALK

1. Walk along Sugar Lane and just before a sharp left bend go up some steps and over a stile on the left into a field. Carry on along the right-hand side of two fields to footbridges over a stream. Over the bridges follow a clear path steeply up the hillside for about 150 yards to a cross path.

2. Turn left to a gate. Immediately after the gate bear right uphill to a ladder stile by a gate. Through the gate, press on along a delightful level path for about half a mile. (Note: there are many paths up onto the ridge but the route described is the easiest, though not the shortest.)

3. Immediately before a wall starts on the right of the path, turn very sharp right, almost back on yourself, uphill on a clear path. Follow this up to and then along the ridge. Continue past a white-painted trig point to a complex stile giving onto a cross path.

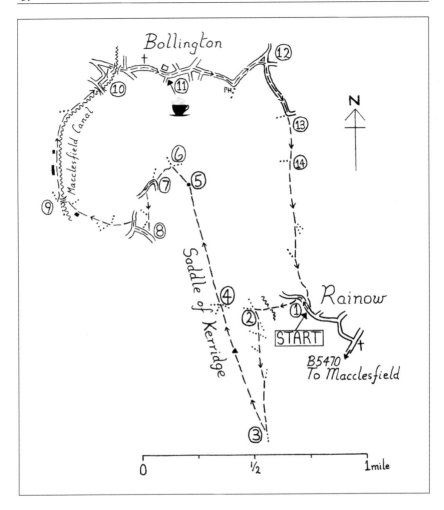

The Kerridge Ridge is an important landscape feature, with spectacular views across the Cheshire Plain and towards the Peak District. If you look down the western slopes you will see that it has been extensively quarried. Extraction started in 1515 when Henry VIII granted Macclesfield Corporation the right to work the stone. They promptly paved the town with it and word spread that it was a fine, hard wearing but workable stone. There is still some quarrying on a small scale.

4. Turn right to continue along the ridge in the same direction to a curious white monument.

This is White Nancy. It was built by the Gaskell family as a summerhouse to commemorate the battle of Waterloo in 1815. It was white-washed from the beginning, but painted green during the Second World War so as not to provide a landmark for enemy aircraft. It has stone seats and an enormous stone table inside reached through an oak door. The folly's entrance was sealed with the table still inside because of a very real fear that vandals would damage it. There are several explanations for its curious name. One says it comes from the ordnance column that was on the site before the folly and Nancy is a corruption of the 'nance' part of ordnance. Alternatively, Mrs Gaskell, wife of the folly's builder, and her daughter were called Nancy. A third explanation is that the lead horse of a team of eight used to drag heavy building materials uphill, including the table, was also called Nancy. You can take your choice!

5. From the monument take a clear path slightly left and downhill to a track.

6. Turn left over a cattle grid along the track to a lane.

7. Turn right for 150 yards then turn left on a signed path starting over a stepped squeeze stile. Follow the flagged path to a lane.

8. Turn right. At a T-junction turn right for 40 yards then turn left on a signed path along a track. Continue through the gate at Bobbin Cottage to a bridge over a canal on the left.

9. Turn right along the towpath.

This is the Macclesfield Canal (see walk 15, page 72). Adelphi is Greek for brothers and on the left overlooking the canal is Adelphi Mill, built in 1851 by George and Martin Swindells as a cotton mill. The Swindells family was a major force in transforming Bollington from an agricultural village of 1,200 people in 1801 to an industrial town with a population of 4,600 by 1851.

10. Some 50 yards after the first bridge – number 27 – turn left through a gate onto a lane. Now turn immediately right again on a surfaced path in front of a cottage that soon leads down steep steps to a main road. Turn right under an impressive aqueduct and follow the main road to the teashop on the right.

11. Turn right out of the teashop and continue along the main road to a complex junction at a mini-roundabout. Take the second road on the right, Ingersley Road, signed 'Rainow'. Follow this out of Bollington. When this forks, branch right, signed 'Rainow $2^1/_2$'.

Bollington is sometimes known as 'Happy Valley'. There are two explanations for this. The first is that Samuel Gregg, a local entrepreneur, was a philanthropist who valued his workers and tried to improve their living conditions. Gregg called Bollington 'Goldenthal', German for 'Happy Valley'. The alternative is that Bollington has always been a good place to live with full employment and a pub on every corner in its heyday.

12. Turn right along Oakenbank Lane.

13. When the lane bends left, carry on in the same direction, over a stile, down steps into a little valley and up the other side and on to a substantial stone stile.

14. Over the stile go ahead a few feet then cross a stile on the right. Turn immediately left to continue in the same direction as before, now with a wall on the left. Follow the path, not always visible on the ground, from stile to stile, ignoring the more obvious animal tracks that tend to lead from gate to gate. The path eventually becomes a hedged path that leads behind some cottages back to the start in Sugar Lane.

The documented history of Rainow extends back to the 12th century when it was part of the royal hunting forest of Macclesfield and subject to harsh forest law. Major changes came in the late 1700s with the Industrial Revolution. The new turnpike roads improved communication and the invention of textile machinery took home-based cloth making into the 13 water-powered mills, which were eventually built. In the first half of the 19th century Rainow would have been a busy, noisy industrial village of over 1,800 people. The new transport links of canal, then railway, passed Rainow by and people drifted away to the towns. Since then it has been transformed again into a pleasant residential community. Rainow has a mayor. He used to be chosen at Rainow Wakes in October when he was dressed in a red robe, an immense chain of office and a hat with various colours of ribbons and put on a donkey facing the tail end. A procession round the village called at every inn and the mayor was provided with liquid refreshment. The mayor is now invited to the village fete held each June. The fete also continues the local tradition of a running race to the top of Kerridge.

Walk 14
LYME PARK

Cheshire is usually thought of as a county of rich farmland but at its north-eastern fringe it includes part of the Peak District National Park. This is an immensely varied route including a steady moorland climb, which makes it without doubt the most energetic in this book. However, the effort is well worth it with stunning views both west across the sprawl of Manchester and the county beyond and east into the Peak District. Having skirted Lyme Park on the outward leg the route enters the estate and descends across the moor and through woodland for refreshment at a National Trust teashop. Excellent as the walk before tea is, the best is yet to come with a particularly enjoyable stroll down a thickly wooded valley carved by a small stream. One word of warning: you may wish to avoid busy weekends when the area round the teashop and Hall can be very crowded and the starting place may be full.

The Coffee Shop at Lyme Park has an airy, modern interior and a few tables outside. It offers an impressive selection of delicious cakes and scones with jam and cream. Lunches are served from noon to 2.30 pm and include filled jacket potatoes, baguettes and tempting salads as well as soup. It is open between 10.30 am and 5 pm every day in the summer and at weekends in the winter. Telephone: 01663 762023.

DISTANCE: 5 miles.

MAP: OS Explorer 268 Wilmslow, Macclesfield and Congleton.

STARTING POINT: Lay-by opposite Needygate Farm. GR 948816.

HOW TO GET THERE: At the junction of the A523 and A5149 at traffic lights in Poynton take a road east for about $2^1/_4$ miles. Follow the signs towards Pott Shrigley and continue through a tunnel under a canal. The lay-by is on the left after a further quarter of a mile.

ALTERNATIVE STARTING POINT: If you wish to visit the teashop at the beginning or end of your walk, start in the main car park for Lyme Park where there is ample parking (charge). You will then start the walk at point 9.

THE WALK

1. With your back to the entrance to Needygate Farm go through a wooden kissing gate at the right-hand end of the lay-by. Follow the path to a lane.

2. Turn right.

3. At a Methodist chapel turn left up a track. Fork right at Hillside Cottage and soon the track becomes a path. Carry on along the path, never far from the wall of Lyme Park on the left, to a stile by a gate onto a track.

The square tower you can see within Lyme Park on your left is Lyme Cage. It was built in the 17th century as an observation tower for watching the progress of the hunt and was later used as a lock-up for poachers. It has recently been restored and decorated as it would have been in 1815. The route does not pass it but it is open to the public.

4. Turn right.

5. Immediately after passing Keepers Cottage turn left on a path signed 'To Bowstonegates and Kettleshulme'. Walk up beside a rather broken wall, not forgetting to admire the widening view behind you as you climb up the slope to a stile. From the stile, go ahead to a gate across a track.

6. Turn left along the track and follow it to a T-junction with a cross track.

7. Turn left to Bowstones Farm.

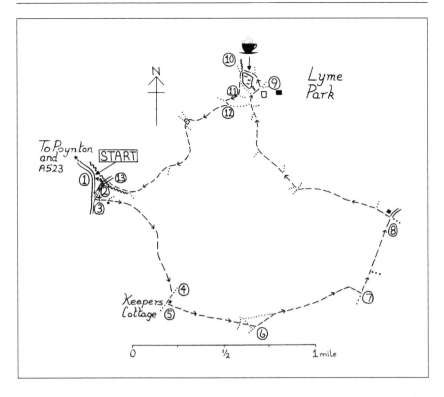

8. Go over a stile to the left of the entrance to Bowstones Farm and walk with a fence on the right to a tall ladder stile giving access to Lyme Park. Follow the track ahead to eventually reach a ladder stile by a gate into a wood. Over this stile continue in the same direction through the wood ignoring all side paths. Leave the wood at yet another ladder stile and press on along the track, which leads to the main car park and visitor centre.

Lyme Park is essentially a medieval deer park of almost 1,400 acres of moor, woods and parkland where herds of red and fallow deer still roam. It belonged to the Legh family from the 14th century until 1946 when Robert Legh inherited it and promptly gave it to the National Trust. A phantom funeral procession is said to haunt the park and especially the woods the route goes through. It is a ghostly re-enactment of the funeral cortege of Sir Piers Legh, who died in Paris on 16th June 1422, of wounds sustained in the Battle of Meux. A 'Lady in White' follows the procession at a distance. This is supposed to be his mistress, Blanche, who was not allowed to attend the funeral and died of grief a few weeks later.

69

9. Turn left by a small lake to the teashop at the far end.

This magnificent house, the largest in Cheshire, was originally a modest hunting lodge. Development started in earnest in the 16th century. Sir Piers Legh VII instigated an extensive rebuilding programme that successive generations added to as fashions changed so it has elements from many eras. The grandeur of the interior includes ceiling paintings by Leoni, a substantial collection of English clocks, priceless Mortlake tapestries, as well as plaster casts of Greek friezes showing battle scenes, brought here by Thomas Legh, an intrepid explorer and collector, and Grinling Gibbon's famous woodcarvings. Throughout its long occupation by the Legh family, Lyme Park has certainly witnessed some interesting characters and events. There have been competent businessmen, valiant soldiers, influential MPs and diplomats, not forgetting one of the more colourful members of the family who made his claim to fame as an Egyptologist and their lives are reflected in the contents. The house is surrounded by 17 acres of Victorian gardens that boast impressive bedding schemes, a sunken parterre, an Edwardian rose garden, Jekyll-style herbaceous borders, a reflection lake, a ravine garden and a conservatory. The house and garden are open from the end of March to end of October, Friday to Tuesday from 1 pm to 5 pm and on Bank Holiday Mondays from 11 am to 5 pm. Telephone: 01663 766492.

10. From the teashop continue on the path round the lake. Some 10 yards after a bench overlooking the lake bear right on a small path leading uphill through trees.

Lyme Park provided the exterior shots of 'Pemberley', home of Mr Darcy in the BBC TV production of Pride and Prejudice. *The small lake was the scene of his swim. According to the National Trust the number of visitors to Lyme Park rose by 178 per cent after the broadcast.*

11. In front of a high deer fence turn right and follow the path up to a track. Turn left to shortly reach a surfaced drive.

12. Turn right and follow the drive to a small car park. Go through the gate at the far end of the car park and continue on a track down a beautiful valley to a gate onto a lane.

13. Turn left for 20 yards then take a path on the right to retrace your steps to the start. (If you started at Lyme Park, continue along the lane to pick up the route at point 3.)

Walk 15
MACCLESFIELD CANAL AND THE MIDDLEWOOD WAY

This walk makes use of the arteries of our industrial past - a canal and an amenity path developed from a disused railway - now given over to recreation. The demands of the technology that initially developed these routes means that they are almost completely level and I have never done a walk with so many seats to rest and watch the antics of the canal life, both human and avian. Put that together with two possible tea stops and you have the ideal walk for a lazy day.

The first tea stop is Lyme View Café on the Macclesfield Canal. Geared to meet the needs of the canal community, the substantial breakfast is an important part of the menu. For lunch there is a selection of sandwiches, salads and filled jacket potatoes as well as more sustaining suggestions from the daily specials board. Tea is not neglected with a choice of cakes, scones or toasted teacakes. There are some tables outside on a veranda. They are

71

open Tuesday to Saturday from 9.30 am. Telephone 01625 850985. The Coffee Tavern at Higher Poynton is a few yards off the route. It is decorated with entertaining murals painted by an artist from the canal and has a shady garden. It serves snacks and full lunches as well as scones and some cakes. Open every day except Monday. Telephone: 01625 874315.

DISTANCE: $4^1/_2$ miles.

MAP: OS Explorer 268 Wilmslow, Macclesfield and Congleton.

STARTING POINT: Jacksons Brickworks car park. GR 947843.

HOW TO GET THERE: From the A6, Stockport–Disley road, about a mile east of Hazel Grove take a minor road south, Norbury Hollow Road. This is unsigned but is just east of the Robin Hood. Follow this for about a mile then turn left along Pool House Road, signed 'Middlewood Way Jacksons Brickworks'.

ALTERNATIVE STARTING POINT: If you wish to visit the teashop at the beginning or end of your walk, there is a car park at Lyme View Café and permission should be sought before leaving a car. You will then start the walk at point 3. Alternatively, park at Nelson Pit Visitor Centre on the Middlewood Way. Turn right out of the car park and left along Shrigley Road North to the Coffee Tavern on the right. You will then start the walk at point 4.

THE WALK

1. Go to the far right-hand side of the car park to find a footpath. After 50 yards turn right, signed 'To Canal', to a track. Turn left and follow the track to a cross track and through a gate to the canalside.

2. Turn right along the towpath and follow it for 2 miles to the first opportunity for tea, beside the canal, just before bridge number 18. Immediately before the bridge turn right off the towpath and right along a lane for 70 yards to the entrance to Lyme View Café.

The Macclesfield Canal cost £320,000 and was built at the end of the canal age to serve the now disused coal fields at Adlington and Poynton and the mill towns of Bollington, Macclesfield and Congleton where fine cotton and silk manufacturing were the principal industries. In the 1850s manure from Manchester Corporation stables and 'night soil' from cess-pits were transported to be sold to farmers as fertilizer. It opened on 19th November 1831 and some 20,000 people watched the opening procession of boats. According to the local paper ladies were not permitted on the boats because of 'a very natural anxiety for the preservation of their health, which might have been endangered by exposure to the cold and damp atmosphere'. Commercial traffic carried

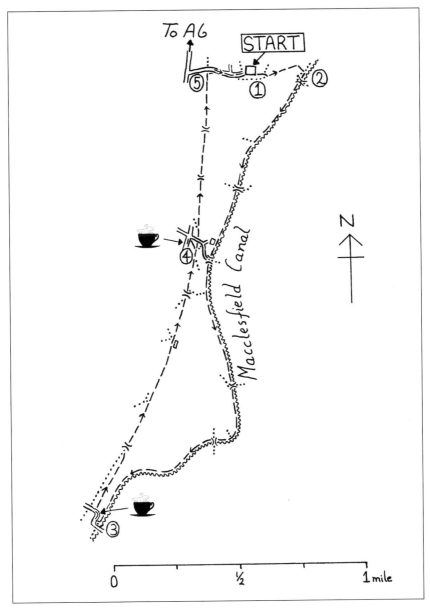

on until the 1960s. Milestones were placed by the canal for the collection of tolls of one to two pennies a mile. The milestones were buried or had their mileages obliterated during the Second World War to prevent enemy soldiers using them as an aid to navigation. They were restored in the 1980s by the Macclesfield Canal Society. The canal travels through some very picturesque landscapes and is part of the popular Cheshire ring.

3. Return to the lane and turn immediately right on a path signed 'Middlewood Way'. Follow the path along the top of a cutting then press ahead in the same direction when it joins the path in the bottom. Carry on past a car park at Poynton Copse.

The Middlewood Way is a former railway linking Marple with Macclesfield and was sold by British Railways for £1. It was built as a result of pressure from mill owners in Bollington and pit owners in Poynton during a time of economic depression to improve the distribution of coal and bring down costs. The railway opened on 2nd August 1869 and within a week of opening the line ran an excursion to Manchester from Macclesfield for 600 passengers. Despite this enthusiasm, the line always struggled to make a profit and closed in 1970.

4. At a picnic site at an old station bear left up to a road and turn left a few yards to the second opportunity for tea on the right. Return to the Middlewood Way and continue in the same direction under the bridge at the end of the old platform.

After the closure of the railway, the line became derelict until Macclesfield and Stockport Council reopened the route again as the Middlewood Way. Wild animal and plant populations can come under threat when urban development splits them up into small islands, each too small to be viable. Areas such as this are very important for conservation because they act as corridors, linking one population with another.

5. Immediately before the third bridge after the old station and picnic site, turn right on a path up to a road. Turn right back to the car park where this walk started.

Walk 16
HARE HILL AND ALDERLEY EDGE

This delightful walk explores Alderley Edge, one of Cheshire's favourite beauty spots. It is now owned and managed by the National Trust and covered in magnificent mixed woodland making a visit a pleasure at any time of year. The route starts at Hare Hill, another National Trust property well worth a visit in its own right. It uses a permissive path that crosses mature, rolling parkland before entering the woods. A steep climb brings you to the main viewpoint but there are many other wonderful vistas along the way. A short stroll leads to the famous tearoom. The return leg is an easy amble using well maintained paths and drives with more excellent views across to the Peak District hills.

The Wizard Tea Room has been deservedly popular with generations of walkers at Alderley Edge and occupies a simple stone building next to the National Trust information centre. There are some tables inside, made cosy in winter by a wood-burning stove, and more outside. There is a superb selection of cakes served in generous slices. For lunch, toasted sandwiches, filled jacket potatoes or a hearty soup supplement these and all offer excellent value for money. They are open between 11 am and 4 pm on Saturday and Sunday and Bank Holidays throughout the year. Telephone: 01625 584412. There is no other source of refreshment on this walk.

DISTANCE: 4 miles.
MAP: OS Explorer 268 Wilmslow, Macclesfield and Congleton.
STARTING POINT: National Trust car park at Hare Hill (charge). GR 876766.
HOW TO GET THERE: From the B5087 Alderley Edge–Macclesfield road 2 miles from
   Alderley Edge town, take a minor road signed 'Prestbury' for three-quarters of a
   mile to the entrance drive to Hare Hill on the left.
ALTERNATIVE STARTING POINT: If you wish to visit the teashop at the beginning or
   end of your walk, start in the National Trust car park (charge) on the B5087. The
   teashop is adjacent to the car park. You will then start the walk at point 9.

THE WALK
Hare Hill is a fine Victorian woodland garden, with a delightful walled garden at its heart, containing a pergola and wire sculptures. During early summer Hare Hill offers a blaze of colour from its large collection of rhododendrons and azaleas. The garden appeals to other senses too, with the air full of bird song and heavy with the sweet fragrance from the numerous blooms. The garden is open from 10 am until 5.30 pm Wednesday, Thursday, Saturday and Sunday between early April and the end of October and every day in May when the floral display is at its best. Telephone 01625 584412.

1. Go to the centre rear of the car park to find a permissive path signed 'Alderley Edge'. Follow the waymarks across parkland and through a wood to a T-junction with a cross path.

2. Turn left. Go over a stile out of the wood and press on over a cross track. Follow the path round to the left at the end of the field to find another stile on the right into more woodland.

3. Follow the path up through the wood to a stile for the first of the many views from the Edge. Go ahead for 30 yards to a fork.

The Edge, which rises to more than 600 feet, was formed more than 200 million years ago by an upthrust of red sandstone occurring along a fault line. There are broad views across the Cheshire Plain. The radio telescope at Jodrell Bank stands out clearly to the south-west.

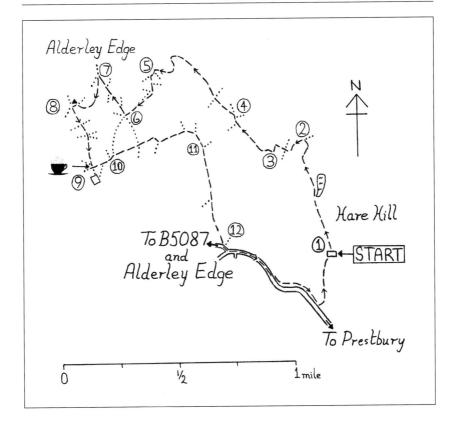

4. Take the left branch through a small gate and up some steps, shortly passing some seats well placed to admire the views. Follow the clear path, eventually dropping down into a small valley.

5. A few yards further on the path forks. Bear left, signed 'The Edge' and follow the path uphill, ignoring paths to left and right to reach a complex junction near the top with two tracks on the left.

'Well, Jack, and where art thou bound to?'
'Dunham'
' Why, what an old-fashioned chap thou be'est. Thy granddad afore thee went to Dunham; but thou wert always a slow coach. I'm off to Alderley - me and my missus.'
     So did two textile workers discuss a day out in the 1840s in Mrs Gaskell's 'Libby Marsh's Three Eras'. *The recently-opened Birmingham and*

Manchester Railway had a stopping place close to the Edge and ran cheap excursions in Whit Week. Lord Stanley, the landowner, allowed the great British public to visit the beauty spot, which they have been doing in large numbers ever since. This invasion was not universally well received. Lady Stanley referred to the visitors as 'Cottentots' and complained that one could 'neither handcuff nor great dog them if they are intrusive or offensive'.

6. Turn right to a rocky outcrop and viewpoint.

This is Stormy Point. The holes in the ground are old mine workings (there are no natural caves at Alderley Edge) and the ground has been laid bare by the mine waste and the tramping of thousands of feet. One mine is called Devil's Grave and it is said that if you walk round it seven times reciting the Lord's Prayer backwards the Devil will appear.

7. From here, two other paths lead to the left, back into the wood. Take the first one and walk to a mound topped by a low stone plinth.

In 1588 this was the site of a beacon to warn of the approach of the Spanish Armada. In those days the Edge was covered in grass and heather so it would have been clearly seen for miles around. The original building was a small room in which an iron pot filled with pitch was kept. The building was replaced in 1779 and kept in readiness during the Napoleonic Wars. It was destroyed in a gale in 1931.

8. Follow the path sharply round to the left, taking a path with a wheelchair waymark. Continue ahead over a cross path to a cross track and the tearoom on the right.

The path passes Engine Vein, the site of the largest of the copper mines on Alderley Edge. Veins of copper, iron and lead were found in the sandstone and are thought to have been worked in prehistoric times. In the middle of the 18th century the mines were relatively prosperous, one of them employing 50 men. The last mine closed shortly after the end of the First World War.

9. Turn left out of the tearoom along a track for about 250 yards.

According to tradition, once upon a time, a farmer from Mobberley, mounted on a white horse, was crossing the Edge on his way to Macclesfield to sell the animal. He was startled by the sudden appearance of a tall old man strangely clad in a deep flowing garment. The old man ordered him to stop and offered to buy the horse. The farmer, however, refused the offer, not thinking it sufficient. 'Go, then, to Macclesfield,' said the old man, 'but mark my words, you will not sell the horse. Should you find my words come true, meet me this evening, and I will buy your horse.' To his great surprise, and greater disappointment, nobody would buy, though all admired his beautiful horse. On his way home he saw the old man again, who commanded him, 'Follow me!' The old man touched a rock with a wand, and immediately the farmer saw a huge pair of iron gates, which flew open with a sound like thunder. 'Fear nothing,' spoke the Wizard, 'and behold a sight which no mortal eye has ever looked upon.' The farmer saw a countless number of men and white horses, all fast asleep. Heaps of treasure were piled up on the ground. From these the old man told the farmer to take the money for his horse, and said: 'You see these men and horses; the number was not complete. Your horse was wanted to make it complete. Remember my words, there will come a day when these men and these horses, awakening from their enchanted slumber, will descend into the plain, decide the fate of a great battle, and save their country. Henceforward no mortal eye will ever look upon the iron gates. Be gone!'

This story is of great antiquity and in England can be traced back to at least Roman times as Plutarch mentions it. It occurs in various forms throughout Europe and much of Asia always associated with local heroes. The legend of the Wizard of Alderley Edge first appeared in print in the Manchester Mail of 1805, reported by a correspondent who obtained it from a local man Thomas Broadhurst, better known as Old Daddy. During the Second World War, at a time of threatened invasion, the people of Alderley revealed that their belief was not entirely dead. It was often said, mainly in jest, that it was time for the knights to wake up. And they'd better not take their white horses with them, but get themselves some white tanks instead.

10. When the track bends left turn right on a fenced path. Cross a track and continue ahead. Follow the path round to the right to a stile by a gate onto a track that ends in two stiles. Go over the one on the right and follow the fenced path to another stile.

11. Over this stile turn right to reach a farm drive. Turn right along the drive to a road.

12. Turn left. At a T-junction after 50 yards turn left again. Eventually, a stile on the left gives access to a permissive path parallel with the road. Follow this to the drive to Hare Hill and turn left back to the car park where this walk started.

Walk 17
KNUTSFORD AND TATTON PARK

*T*his *exceptionally interesting walk starts in Knutsford and explores the woods and mere close to the town before entering Tatton Park. Cheshire County Council now manages this for the people of the county and there is no entrance fee for pedestrians, only for cars. It passes many of the main sites including the Old Hall, Airborne Forces memorial and the mansion and gardens before a welcome refreshment break at the extensive stable-yard. The route is fairly level but it is not particularly short so you really need to allow a full day if you wish to include a visit to either of the halls or the magnificent gardens. The walk perhaps saves the best till last: the return is an easy stroll along a superb mature beech avenue with extensive views.*

 The Stables Restaurant is housed in converted stables and has an airy, modern interior as well as plenty of tables outside in the yard itself. There is an outstanding selection of wickedly tempting cakes and pastries. Can you justify such an indulgence on an easy, more or less level walk? Of course you can! Possibilities for lunch range from full meals, with a daily choice of specials such as venison sausages with onion gravy, through jacket potatoes to some innovative pannini, for example on my visit chicken with olive and ginger marmalade. They are open all day every day in the summer and just close on Monday in winter. Telephone: 01625 534421.

DISTANCE: 5½ miles.

MAP: OS Explorer 268 Wilmslow, Macclesfield and Congleton.

STARTING POINT: Tatton Street car park, Knutsford. GR 751789.

HOW TO GET THERE: From the junction of the A50 and A5033 at Knutsford, take the road into the town centre and follow it round to the left to a car park on the left.

ALTERNATIVE STARTING POINT: If you wish to visit the teashop at the beginning or end of your walk, start in Tatton Park at the main car park for the mansion and gardens. There is a parking charge for cars. You will then start the walk at point 9.

THE WALK

1. Return to the road and take a path next to house number 45 across a small open area. Cross a road and continue ahead along Drury Lane. Shortly, bear right at the fork to stay on Drury Lane. Follow it round to the right as it becomes more of a track.

2. Just before the track becomes a road again turn left on a surfaced path that leads by a mere.

Unlike many of Cheshire's meres, Tatton Mere is not a natural feature. It was created in medieval times when a river was dammed to form the lake. It is home to many species of birds and a plaque helps identify what you see.

3. When the railings on the left end, turn left and follow the main path through a wood to a stile. (Ignore a stile on the left some 25 yards before.) Go ahead for 30 yards to a fork and bear right to continue through the woods to meet a major track.

4. Turn left to shortly reach a gate into Tatton Park. Through the gate bear left to walk beside Tatton Mere. When the path forks at the end of a high deer fence on the right, bear right to carry on by the mere on a slightly higher-level path. Press on round the mere to meet a roughly surfaced track.

81

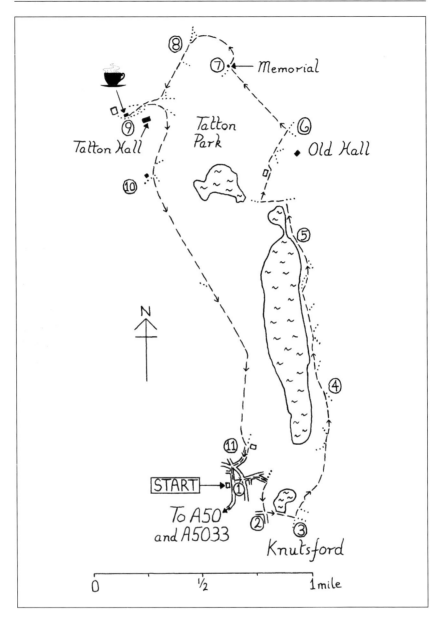

Tatton is one of the most complete historic estates in Britain. The Egerton family acquired it in 1598 and owned it until the childless Maurice,

Baron Egerton of Tatton, bequeathed it to the National Trust in 1958 for the benefit of the Nation'. Tatton Park spans 2,000 acres, with 1,000 acres of deer park and 50 acres of gardens. It is managed, maintained and financed by Cheshire County Council on behalf of the National Trust. The park attracts over 700,000 visitors each year and is host to over 70 events annually, notably the Royal Horticulture Society Flower Show and the Halle Fireworks and Light spectacular.

5. Turn right along the track to a T-junction with a surfaced drive. Turn left for 150 yards then right along another surfaced drive, signed 'Old Hall Landscape History Trail Melchett Walk'. Carry on past a car park on the left and the Old Hall on the right.

Tatton is probably named after a Saxon lord called Tata. There seems to have been a manor house on the site of the Old Hall since the Saxon period and a village grew up around it and along the road to Knutsford. The Egertons eventually moved across the park to their new hall, leaving the Old Hall to be converted into workers' cottages. There are regular tours that guide you through its long history and displays to give a glimpse of life during the many centuries people have lived here. (Telephone: 01625 534400 for dates and times.) When the parkland was laid out, the village was thought to be an eyesore and was cleared away.

6. At a track on the right and information board about Tatton at war on the right, turn left on an ill-defined path across parkland and go directly ahead to find a memorial to the air-borne forces who trained at Tatton. This is a low stone column in a small enclosure and there is a seat in front of it, well placed to admire the views to the east across to the Peak District.

7. Turn right to pick up a track and follow it round to the left to meet the entrance drive.

8. Turn left and walk beside the drive to Tatton Hall. At the end of the mansion turn left through metal gates then bear right to the stable-yard and teashop.

Tatton Hall is the jewel in the estate's crown. The state rooms and most of the family rooms still contain the paintings, furnishings and contents purchased by the Egerton family over a period of some 200 years, including the original furniture designed for them by the renowned cabinet makers, Gillows of Lancaster and London. A guidebook gives full details of each room, the Egerton family and their collections. Perhaps even more interesting are the extensive servants' quarters giving a glimpse of life below stairs that would have been the lot of most of us. The Hall is open during the afternoons except Monday in summer and guided tours are available. (Telephone: 01625 534400 for dates and times.)

9. Retrace your steps past the hall but now bear right on a path by a fence round the gardens. Follow this as far as a low concrete wall on the left then fork right, up to an avenue of magnificent beeches leading from an ornamental 'temple' at the end of the gardens.

If the Hall is the jewel in the crown then the gardens are the superb setting and well worth a visit if you have time. Tatton's gardens are a collection of gardens within a garden, with an 18th-century orangery and fernery comprising part of a collection of glasshouses. The fernery was designed in the late 1850s by Joseph Paxton and provided Lord Egerton with a showcase for his collection of Australian and New Zealand tree ferns, which is now of national significance. There are Italian and rose gardens as well as Tatton's unique Japanese garden. The reason for this variety is that when the Egerton family decided to develop a new garden to reflect the latest horticultural whim or fashion, they simply converted more of the park into garden by moving the boundary fence rather than redeveloping an existing garden. The gardens are open Tuesday to Sunday (plus bank holidays) all year except Christmas Day.

10. Turn left and enjoy this magnificent path for $1\frac{1}{2}$ miles until it joins an entrance drive near a classical arch.

11. Turn right and leave Tatton Park through the arch. Follow the path by the drive round to the right to a road. Cross the road and go ahead along Tatton Street to the car park.

Knutsford is Mrs Gaskell's famous 'pleasant little country town of Cranford'. The town's most illustrious daughter came to live with her aunt on the death of her mother in 1810 when she was barely a month old. Admired for both her talent and beauty, she married a Unitarian minister and wrote many novels as well as Charlotte Brontë's biography but she is best remembered for her kindly and humorous depiction of country-town life among the impoverished gentility.

Walk 18
DUNHAM MASSEY

This route is a gentle, level amble but has much of interest to see on the way, exploring Dunham Massey estate, visiting two estate villages and the Bridgewater canal. It is unusual for this book in two ways. Firstly, only a short stretch lies within the boundaries of modern Cheshire, the rest being in Greater Manchester. Since I feel it is unlikely that I will write a book of walks in Greater Manchester, I do not want to let the stroke of a civil servant's pen exclude it. Secondly, since there is now no other parking in the vicinity, it starts and finishes very close to the teashop.

The Stables Restaurant is on the upper floor above the shop and occupies a surprisingly long room with a beamed ceiling and exposed brick walls. It offers the excellent fare we expect from National Trust tearooms, including a tempting selection of cakes or scones with jam and cream. A tasty alternative is a Cheshire cheese and herb scone. For a light lunch there are well-filled sandwiches, salads and jacket potatoes and those

85

with a heartier appetite are catered for by daily specials such as a spiced lamb and apricot casserole which I sampled on my visit. It is open from 10.30 am throughout the year until 5 pm in the summer and 4 pm between the end of October and the end of March. Telephone: 0161 9412815.

Delicious ice cream is available from the kiosk at the mill end of the stable block.

DISTANCE: 4¹/₂ miles.

MAP: OS Explorer 276 Bolton, Wigan and Warrington.

STARTING POINT: Dunham Massey car park (charge unless you are a member of the National Trust). GR 732875.

HOW TO GET THERE: The entrance is on the B5160, signed from the A56, about a mile south-west of Altrincham.

THE WALK

1. Facing the entrance to the car park, go to the right and take a drive past a lake and the stable block housing the tea room to the mill.

At the time of Domesday, Dunham belonged to the Masseys and there was a castle here. The lake might well have been part of the moat. In the early 15th century it passed to the Booths by marriage and there was a splendid Elizabethan mansion on this site. This was demolished and the present building completed in 1740 by George Booth, second Earl of Warrington. Both his father and grandfather had been heavily involved in the turbulent politics of the 17th century, on the Parliament side during the Civil War. When he inherited, in 1694, the estate was heavily in debt and he spent all of his life ensuring he would leave things in a much better state including marriage to a London heiress he had never met. His only child, a daughter, married a member of the Grey family, the Earl of Stamford. Even earlier than the Booths' political career the Grey family had tragically involved themselves in the struggle for power in late Tudor times. The sad tale of Lady Jane Grey, queen for nine days, was only one example of the Grey family history. When the estate was bequeathed to the National Trust in 1976, it was one of the most generous the Trust was granted. The house is renowned as one of Britain's most sumptuous Edwardian interiors, with exceptional collections of 18th-century walnut furniture, paintings and Huguenot silver, as well as extensive servants' quarters. It is open to the public from noon, Saturday to Wednesday between late March and early November. (Telephone: 0161 9411025.)

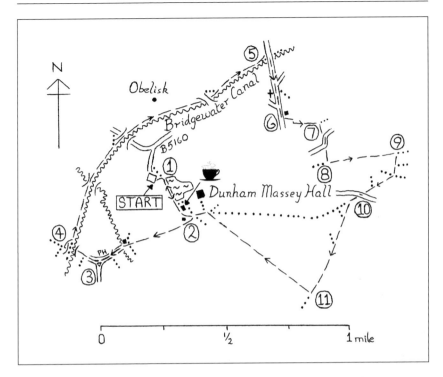

2. Go past the mill and turn right to a stile by a gate. Over the stile, follow the track ahead to a lane. Walk in front of Bollington Mill and continue ahead into Little Bollington. Go ahead along a lane past the Swan With Two Nicks pub.

The mill, which has recently been restored, dates from the same period as the earlier mansion, both built by Sir George Booth around the time of the Armada.

The river you crossed is the Bollin, the boundary between Greater Manchester and Cheshire. Documentary evidence from the 14th century shows there were ' eel traps ' and ' fish lepes'. There has probably been a mill here since the 13th century but the present building is about 150 years old and has been converted to luxury flats.

3. At a junction bear right and the road shortly becomes a cobbled track. Follow this to a tunnel under a canal.

4. At the far end of the tunnel turn right up to the canal path and turn left beside the canal. Continue over an aqueduct over the river Bollin and a second aqueduct over a lane almost as far as the second bridge over the canal.

This is the Bridgewater Canal (see walk 19, page 92) and in the past many visitors made the excursion to Dunham this way (see walk 16, page 77). The obelisk on the left was erected as a vista point, seen from the house.

5. Some 20 yards before the bridge take a path that leads up to a lane. Turn right along the lane through Dunham Town.

6. Some 25 yards after Dunham Town post office turn left on a path signed 'Oldfield Lane' and follow the hedged path to a fork.

7. Bear right across a field to a stile onto a lane. Turn right for 30 yards then cross a stile on the left to continue in the same direction along the left-hand side of a field to a cross path.

8. Turn left along the right-hand side of a field to a stile onto a golf course. Go more or less straight ahead, negotiating from blue sign to blue sign, to find a path at the edge of a woodland area.

9. Turn right. When the path shortly turns left, go ahead to another blue sign at a cross path. Now bear slightly right to yet another blue sign rather hidden behind a tree at the time of writing. This marks the path off the golf course. Follow this to a road.

10. Cross the road to a stile beside a gate back into Dunham Massey park. Some 25 yards after the stile bear left off the drive onto a path. Follow this path, going through tall deer gates, for a bare half mile to a grassy drive where the wall on the left is replaced by ornamental railings.

The park supports a fine herd of fallow deer and you are likely to see them on this walk. The unusual building on the right is a 200-year-old deer barn. In cold weather the deer will nibble at bark and this can kill saplings. The restoration work being undertaken to the fine trees for which Dunham is famous means that the movements of the deer have to be controlled to some extent.

11. Turn right along the drive. This leads back to the house, stables and teashop. Make your way back to the car park.

Walk 19
LYMM

This charming, short walk explores the environs and centre of Lymm, an historic and very attractive village mentioned in the Domesday Book. It falls naturally into two parts. It starts with a near circuit of Lymm Dam followed by an excursion out to Lymm's little sister, Oughtrington, and a return by England's oldest canal. This latter part is entirely on surfaced paths and tracks so, on its own, makes an excellent pipe opener when the ground is too wet to make other routes a pleasure.

Sexton's is a long-established family bakery that has recently re-organised its premises to include a café in the historic centre of Lymm. The cool, modern interior is also a cyber café so you can check your emails while you enjoy your tea with something chosen from the wide selection of cakes and pastries for sale in the shop. The choice for lunch is tempting with filled barm cakes and croissants, a baked baby Camembert with Sexton's delicious bread or a choice of salads, such as smoked trout or chicken and smoked mozzarella. They are open between 8.30 am and 5 pm every day except Sunday throughout the year. Telephone: 01925 753669.

DISTANCE: 3 miles

MAP: OS Explorer 276 Bolton, Wigan and Warrington.

STARTING POINT: Lymm Dam, where there is roadside parking beside the lake. GR 681869.

HOW TO GET THERE: Lymm Dam is on the A56 Altrincham–Warrington road as it passes through Lymm.

ALTERNATIVE STARTING POINT: If you wish to visit the teashop at the beginning or end of your walk, start in Lymm village where there is ample parking in two signed car parks. The teashop is on Eagle Brow in the centre of the village. You will then start the walk at point 8.

THE WALK

1. Facing the lake turn right and walk to the end of the railings. Turn left, signed 'Crosfield Bridge The Bongs', and follow the path by the lake. When the path forks, bear right, slightly away from the lake, and go ahead on this path to a stone-balustraded bridge.

Until the early 19th century, a stream flowed in a valley next to the church with a path leading down to a footbridge. In 1821 the Warrington and Stockport Turnpike Trust was granted the right to build a road and charge tolls on what is now the A56. Rather than build a bridge across the valley they constructed a dam and the valley flooded forming the lake, known as Lymm Dam.

2. Turn left to cross the bridge. At the end of the bridge, take the path on the left, then immediately turn left down some steps. Continue in the same direction as a major path joins from the right. When the path forks, bear left to stay above the lake and stay on the main path as it veers away from the lake. When this path next forks, bear left down to the lake, then fork right to emerge back on the main road next to a church. Note: there are many paths round the lake. Don't worry about the exact route you take but make your way round the lake to the church.

Round Lymm Dam you will see signs directing you to 'The Bongs'. This sounds unusual but is nothing more exotic than a wood. The name comes from a medieval word meaning 'wooded banks'

The Doomsday Book shows that there was a church on this site in the 11th century, one of only nine mentioned in Cheshire. A Norman church

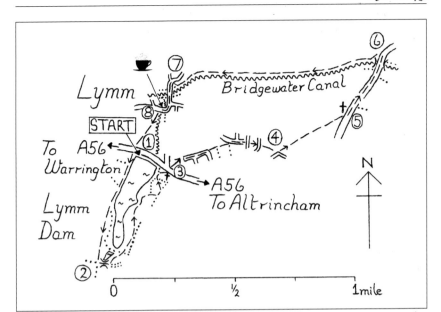

replaced the Saxon one and was itself replaced in the 14th century. The population of Lymm increased rapidly in the 19th century with the coming of better transport links and the church was again rebuilt in 1851 to accommodate this. The tower constructed then was deemed unsafe and was rebuilt in 1889.

3. From the entrance to the church, cross the main road, then turn right to cross Rectory Lane and walk in front of two cottages. Now bear left on a signed path. Continue ahead along a suburban street with houses on the right. When this bends right keep on in the same direction beside playing fields and join a lane. Go past a five-barred gate across the lane, over a road and ahead along a disused lane.

4. When this ends at a road, turn left on a surfaced path signed 'Oughtrington Lane ½'. This path has surprisingly extensive views across the Cheshire plain to the Mersey estuary.

5. At a road turn left, past Oughtrington church, usually closed.

A family, taking their name from the place, lived at Oughtrington Hall as early as the 12th century. This family became extinct through marriage. The name Oughtrington means the 'tun' or farm of the people of 'Uhtred'.

6. Immediately after crossing a canal, turn left down to the towpath, then turn right beside the canal for about a mile.

This is the Bridgewater Canal, sometimes described as England's first canal. The truth of this claim, however, is open to much debate. From Roman times a number of river navigations had been created by constructing weirs and locks. In 1755 it was decided to create river navigation for the Sankey Brook, near Warrington, to carry coal from St Helens down to the River Mersey and Liverpool. Much of the waterway was built as an artificial cut parallel to the river and also using the river in places. While the Sankey was under construction, a few miles to the east, Francis Egerton, the Duke of Bridgewater, was looking for ways to transport coal from his mines at Worsley. The Duke had been to see the Canal du Midi, built in France in 1681, and saw how the Sankey Canal was being built, nearer to home. This gave him the idea to create a waterway that was independent from a river route. In 1758 the Duke called in James Brindley (see walk 12, page 60) to look at ways of constructing a canal and of improving the drainage of the mines. The duke decided to combine the two aims by linking the mines to the canal by an underground canal. This helped drain the mines and provided a source of water for the canal. Commercial traffic continued on the canal until 1974. From 1952, pleasure craft were allowed to use the canal and it became part of the Cheshire Ring circular canal route.

☕ **7.** Just before the first bridge over the canal, bear right to a road and turn left over the canal. Follow the road down into the village, passing Lymm Cross on the left, to the teashop on the right.

Lymm's most famous landmark is the Cross, which is based on ancient steps carved out of the natural red sandstone now worn with age. Four stone pillars support this distinctive landmark that may date back to the 14th century. This was and is the centre of the community and crowds still gather on Christmas Eve to sing carols. Today, Lymm is a most attractive place to live but many industries have flourished in its long history. These include salt production, basket weaving and fustian manufacture. Fustian was a kind of cotton material rather like coarse velvet also known as moleskin. It was used for making working clothes.

8. From the teashop cross the road and take a lane called The Dingle opposite. This shortly becomes a path leading up a steep sided and thickly wooded valley back to the start.

Walk 20
BUDWORTH MERE AND
THE ANDERTON BOAT LIFT

This is a short and easy walk but do allow plenty of time for it because it is crammed with interest – historical, natural and industrial – climaxing in a visit to a marvel of Victorian engineering, now restored to working order. Despite being close to the industrial plant of Northwich, it is also very attractive, with a lovely stretch by Budworth Mere and through woodland as well as a canal-side section. The route also passes the most interesting and beautiful seat it has ever been my privilege to rest upon!

There are two, contrasting, possibilities for tea on this route. The first is Moorings, more of a canal side restaurant than a traditional teashop and serving a wide variety of meals for lunch and dinner to meet the needs of the boating community. The windows overlook Anderton marina, as does the sheltered patio. During the day, hot food is served until 3 pm. Scones

93

and teacakes and desserts to tempt the sweetest of teeth such as blueberry and lemon muffin cake are possibilities for tea. They are open from 11 am every day except Tuesday throughout the year other than the first three weeks in January. Telephone: 01606 79789.

The second option is the café at the modernistic Anderton Boat Lift control centre. This has an outstanding view of the boat lift from its terrace and the building also houses an exhibition about this engineering achievement. They serve a selection of cakes and snacks such as baguettes and an all-day breakfast. They are open every day between 9.45 am and 5 pm. Telephone: 01606 786777.

DISTANCE: 4 miles.

MAP: OS Explorer 267 Northwich and Delamere Forest.

STARTING POINT: Marbury Country Park main car park (charge). GR 652764.

HOW TO GET THERE: From the A559, Warrington–Northwich road, about a mile north-west of Great Budworth take a minor road south, Gibb Hill, signed 'Comberbach Anderton Boat Lift' for about a mile and a half to Marbury Lane and the entrance to the country park. Turn left to the main car park: do not use the parking on Marbury Lane.

ALTERNATIVE STARTING POINT: If you wish to visit the teashop at the beginning or end of your walk, start at Anderton Boat Lift where there is some parking. You will then start the walk at point 6.

THE WALK

The Marbury estate has a history dating back to the 13th century. It is now administered by Cheshire County Council as a country park.

1. Facing the rear of the car park, take a path in the left-hand corner. This shortly leads to a junction of surfaced drives. Turn left then bear right, signed 'Budworth Mere', to pass the public toilets and rangers' office. Continue ahead, signed 'Mere Big Wood', to the mere.

2. Follow the path round to the right by the mere.

One story connected with Marbury is about the Egyptian lover of the heir to the estate. She could not stand the Cheshire weather and went into a decline. Before she died she asked to be buried at Marbury but this was ignored and she was buried at Great Budworth. Her unquiet ghost disturbed the peace and she was returned to Marbury. Her lead-lined coffin was then thrown in the mere but floated ashore. At last she was buried in the rose beds in 1938. When the local press looked into the

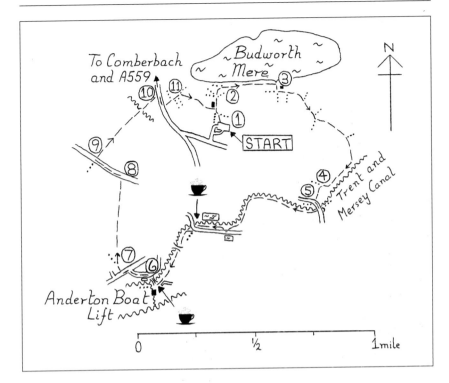

story it turned out that it wasn't a modern person at all but an Egyptian mummy, a common 'ornament' in country houses at one time.

3. At a small inlet follow the main path up a few yards away from the mere to a cross path. Turn left*. When the path forks, bear left, signed 'Anderton Nature Park Canal', soon passing a fantastic seat carved from a single tree trunk and depicting the animals and plants that live in the wood. Eventually the path approaches the canal but shortly veers away again back into the woods.

* In the woods to the left of the path just after you turn left are the remains of an ice house. Blocks of ice were cut in the winter and stored in an underground chamber shaded by trees, They were used to cool iced desserts.

4. Turn left, signed 'Anderton Nature Park' to a stile onto a lane.

5. Turn left over the canal, then go down steps on the left to the canal path and turn left to walk with the canal on your right. At Anderton

95

marina the canal path joins a lane for a few yards before continuing by the canal to the first possibility for tea, reached by leaving the canal path at bridge 198 and turning left over the canal to the teashop on the right. Continue by the canal to the Anderton Boat Lift and the second option for refreshment.

The Anderton Boat Lift was constructed in 1875 so boats could move directly from the Trent and Mersey Canal to the river Weaver 50 feet below. It is a triumph of Victorian engineering. After over 100 years of operation it was found to be unsafe in 1983 and closed. Seventeen years of fund-raising followed to raise the £7 million needed for British Waterways to undertake the painstaking restoration work. The display in the operations centre tells you much more and in the summer you can take a trip on special boats. Telephone: 01606 786777.

6. Cross a footbridge over the canal just before the boat lift. Turn left along a road to a T-junction with a main road.

7. Turn left for 40 yards then right on a signed path leading up to a gate and stile. Go over the stile – not through the gate – and follow the path as it bears right, navigating from stile to stile to a lane.

8. Turn left for about 250 yards.

9. Turn right on a signed path and follow it down across two fields. Carry on along the path through a strip of woodland and along the left-hand side of a third field to the main road.

10. Turn right for 85 yards then left along a surfaced drive to Marbury Hall Nurseries. Ignore the entrance on the right.

11. Take the third small path on the right to an open area with low brick walls. Go across this to pick up a path that emerges by the public toilets and rangers' office. Make your way back to the car park, perhaps diverting right to see the swimming pool or explore the arboretum.

It is thought there have been three halls at Marbury. The low walls show where part of the last house once stood. Built in the 1850s, it was a fine-looking house modelled on Fontainebleau. Between the wars it was a country club and then had various military uses before the barracks were used to house Polish refugees. By 1968 the building had deteriorated to such an extent that it had to be demolished.